THE AUSTRALIAN
Women's Weekly

Sugar FREE

THE AUSTRALIAN WOMEN'S WEEKLY
TRIPLE TESTED
TEST KITCHEN

First published in 2015 by Bounty Books based on materials licensed to it by Bauer Media Books, Australia. Reprinted in 2016.

Bauer Media Books are published by

BAUER MEDIA PTY LIMITED

54 PARK ST, SYDNEY; GPO BOX 4088,

SYDNEY, NSW 2001 AUSTRALIA

phone +61 2 9282 8618; fax +61 2 9126 3702

www.awwcookbooks.com.au

Bauer Media Books

PUBLISHER *Jo Runciman*

EDITORIAL & FOOD DIRECTOR *Pamela Clark*

DIRECTOR OF SALES, MARKETING & RIGHTS *Brian Cearnes*

ART DIRECTOR & DESIGNER *Hannah Blackmore*

SENIOR EDITOR *Stephanie Kistner*

FOOD EDITOR & CONCEPT DIRECTOR *Sophia Young*

OPERATIONS MANAGER *David Scotto*

Printed in China by Leo Paper Products Ltd.

Published and distributed in the
United Kingdom by Bounty Books,
a division of Octopus Publishing Group Ltd
Carmelite House
50 Victoria Embankment
London, EC4Y 0DZ
United Kingdom
info@octopus-publishing.co.uk;
www.octopusbooks.co.uk

International foreign language rights,
Brian Cearnes, Bauer Media Books
bcearnes@bauer-media.com.au

A catalogue record for this book is
available from the British Library.
ISBN: 978-0-7537-2993-9

© Bauer Media Pty Limited 2015

ABN 18 053 273 546

Sugar FREE

Bounty
Books

CONTENTS

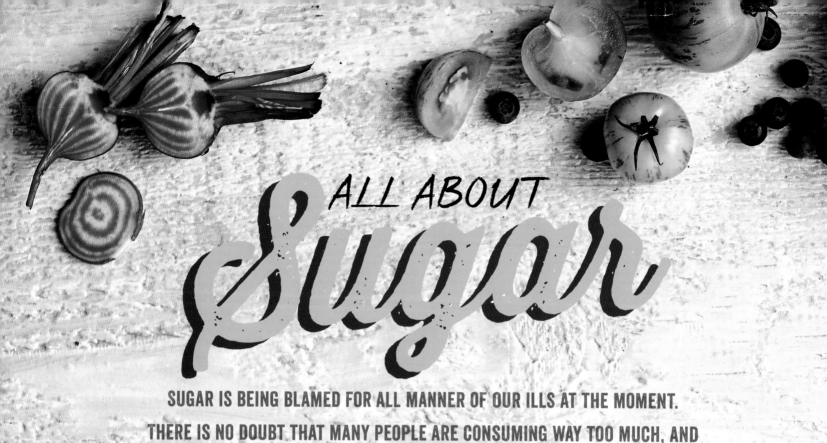

ALL ABOUT
Sugar

SUGAR IS BEING BLAMED FOR ALL MANNER OF OUR ILLS AT THE MOMENT.
THERE IS NO DOUBT THAT MANY PEOPLE ARE CONSUMING WAY TOO MUCH, AND
CERTAINLY SUGAR IS ADDED TO MANY FOODS AND DRINKS, EVEN WHERE YOU WOULD
LEAST EXPECT IT, MAKING IT ALL TOO EASY FOR LEVELS TO SNEAK UP ON YOU.

With the popularity of cutting sugar out of your diet comes much confusion about what exactly sugar is. From a scientific perspective sugars are just the simplest forms of carbohydrates.

All carbohydrates are various combinations of the simplest sugars (mono-saccharides), which include glucose, fructose and galactose. Simple sugars can be joined in pairs to form disaccharides, such as sucrose, or table sugar (glucose and fructose) and lactose (glucose and galactose), the sugar in milk.

Fructose is at the centre of the sugar debate. But, there is a worrying trend that products and recipes that claim to be fructose-free, simply contain other sugars. These other sugars can have a higher GI and have a far greater effect on blood sugar levels than those containing fructose.

Types of sugar

Sugar comes in many guises. When you read the ingredients list of a food product look for syrups including rice malt syrup (brown rice syrup), maltose, molasses, cane juice, coconut sugar, raspadura, maltodextrin, agave syrup and treacle.

Honey and maple syrup are also sugars, although they are not refined as most other sugars are. In fact honey has been a part of human diets since hunter-gatherer days.

But be aware, they are still sugars, and if you have chosen to follow a truly sugar-free diet you'll need to give them a miss.

Natural alternatives to sucrose include sorbitol (commonly used in sugar-free gums and mints), xylitol, stevia or monk fruit (sold as norbu). These are all naturally sweet, provide fewer kilojoules, do not raise blood sugar levels and are tooth friendly. For more information on these and other alternatives, see pages 8 and 9.

Sugar free or not sugar free?

The recipes in this book are free from added refined sugars, including sucrose (table sugar). However, unrefined sugars and sugars naturally present in whole foods are included. There is a big difference between eating whole foods, such as fruits and vegetables, that naturally contain sugars, and foods that have high levels of added refined sugars. Whole foods are rich in fibre and contain a host of antioxidants, vitamins, minerals and phytonutrients that are beneficial for our health. They are worthy of a place in our diet.

Making the change

The word of caution however, is that you don't become so fixated with sugar that you forget to step back and look at your total diet. There are many aspects of diet that are important, and blaming just one thing is dangerous as it blinds us to other, just as important, aspects. Instead, focus on reducing or, if you like, completely cutting out foods with added refined sugars – starting with the obvious no-nos such are lollies, confectionery, biscuits, cakes and sugar-sweetened soft drinks, as they contain little or no nutritional value at all.

The recipes in this book cover all manner of everyday dishes where refined sugars are often unnecessarily present – from the obvious baked goodies to the not-so-obvious marinades, salad dressings and savoury sauces. Using unrefined alternatives and whole foods we've developed scrumptious breakfasts, drinks, main meals and sweet treats the entire family will love – and they won't even notice what's missing.

Sugar ALTERNATIVES

Barley malt syrup

Barley malt syrup is made from sprouted (malted) barley, and produced in a similar way to rice malt syrup.

This dark brown, unrefined sweetener, is thick and sticky with a distinct "malty" flavour, but is not as sweet as honey or table (white) sugar. Barley malt syrup is low in glucose, fructose and sucrose. It is available from health food stores.

Rice malt syrup
(BROWN RICE SYRUP)

Rice malt syrup is made by cooking brown rice flour with enzymes to break down the starch into sugars. The mixture is then filtered and the water removed to give a thick, sweet-tasting syrup. It is available from most major supermarkets and health food stores. Rice malt syrup is fructose-free and is a popular vegan alternative to honey.

Norbu
(MONK FRUIT SUGAR)

Monk fruit is a subtropical melon that has been grown for hundreds of years in South-East Asia. The fruit contains a group of sweet tasting antioxidant compounds. A little like stevia, these compounds deliver sweetness without the sugar and kilojoules. Monk fruit sugar has 96% fewer kilojoules than sugar, and will not affect blood glucose or insulin levels.

Honey
(RAW)

Honey is one of the most natural sweeteners we can use. And since honey bees make honey using the nectar from flowers, the local flora makes an impact on the flavour of the honey. Pure floral honeys have a low GI, but cheaper, blended honeys tend to be high. For a low GI honey look for Yellow Box, Stringy Bark, Red Gum, Iron Bark, Yapunya, Eucalypt or those labelled as pure floral honey.

Agave syrup
(AGAVE NECTAR)

Agave syrup is a sweetener produced from the agave plant (a succulent with thick fleshy leaves) in South Africa and Mexico. It has a low GI due to the high percentage of fructose present, which may be harmful if consumed in high quantities. Sweeter and slightly thinner than honey, agave syrup is another suitable vegan substitute for honey.

Stevia

Stevia comes from the leaves of a plant, so is promoted as a natural sweetener. It is hard to buy stevia in the traditional leaf form. Instead it is processed into a white powder that can be used in a similar way to sugar, a product which is highly refined. It has a minimal effect on blood glucose levels and has no kilojoules, so it can be a useful way to reduce your sugar intake.

Maple syrup
(PURE MAPLE SYRUP)

Pure maple syrup is the concentrated sap of the maple tree, whereas maple-flavoured syrups are usually just processed glucose syrup with added flavourings. Real maple syrup is much tastier and contains significant amounts of nutrients and antioxidant compounds. It has a low GI, making it a good choice for blood glucose control.

Coconut sugar
(COCONUT PALM SUGAR)

Coconut sugar is not made from coconuts, but from the sap of the blossoms of the coconut palm tree. The sap is collected and then boiled to evaporate the water content, leaving a sugar that looks a little like raw or light brown sugar with a similar caramel flavour. It also has the same amount of kilojoules as regular table (white) sugar.

POWER STARTS

CHIA & ALMOND
TOASTED MUESLI

PREP + COOK TIME 20 MINUTES (+ COOLING)
SERVES 4 (MAKES 2 CUPS)

1 cup (90g) rolled oats

2 tablespoons chia seeds

⅓ cup (55g) coarsely chopped almonds

½ teaspoon mixed spice

1 tablespoon pure maple syrup

2 tablespoons sunflower seeds

2 tablespoons LSA (see tips)

1 Preheat oven to 200°C/400°F. Grease and line an oven tray with baking paper.
2 Combine oats, chia, almonds and mixed spice on tray. Drizzle with syrup; toss well.
3 Bake muesli for 10 minutes or until mixture is browned lightly. Cool on tray.
4 Transfer cooled muesli to a medium bowl, add seeds and LSA; stir to combine.

nutritional count per serving 16.5g total fat (1.4g saturated fat); 1104kJ (264 cal); 18.2g carbohydrate; 8.2g protein; 5.2g fibre

tips LSA is a ground mixture of linseeds, sunflower seeds and almonds. It is available from supermarkets and health food stores. You can make double or triple the recipe. Store it in an airtight container in the fridge for up to 3 months.

serving suggestion Serve topped with kiwifruit, banana, strawberries and yoghurt.

MUESLI WITH POACHED PEARS & SHEEP'S MILK YOGHURT

PREP + COOK TIME 45 MINUTES SERVES 6

Eating a healthy breakfast with a good mix of slow-release carbs and protein will help to keep your blood sugar levels in check for the rest of the day. You can skip the poached pear part of this recipe if you like, and top with a mix of fresh or frozen berries instead.

⅓ cup (95g) almond butter

⅓ cup (80ml) pure maple syrup

2 cups (180g) rolled oats

1 cup (50g) flaked coconut

½ cup (80g) flaked almonds

¼ cup (50g) pepitas (pumpkin seeds)

¼ cup (35g) sunflower seeds

¼ cup (20g) quinoa flakes

¼ cup (35g) rolled amaranth or rolled rye

2 tablespoons black or white chia seeds

1 cup (160g) dried sweetened cranberries

6 small corella pears (600g)

2 cups (500ml) apple juice

2 cups (500ml) water

1½ cups (420g) sheep's milk yoghurt

2 tablespoons raw honey or pure maple syrup

1 Preheat oven to 160°C/325°F. Line a large roasting pan with baking paper.

2 Stir almond butter and syrup in a small saucepan over low heat just until combined.

3 Combine oats, coconut, almonds, pepitas, sunflower seeds, quinoa and amaranth in a large bowl. Pour syrup mixture over dry ingredients; working quickly, stir to coat ingredients in syrup mixture.

4 Spread muesli, in an even layer, in pan. Bake 15 minutes. Remove from oven; stir well. Bake for a further 5 minutes or until oats are golden. Cool for 10 minutes; stir in chia seeds and cranberries.

5 Meanwhile, peel, halve and core pears, leaving stalks intact. Place pears in a medium saucepan with juice and the water; bring to the boil. Reduce heat to low; cover pears with a round of baking paper, simmer for 8 minutes or until tender.

6 Place yoghurt and honey in a small bowl; stir gently to swirl through.

7 Serve muesli topped with poached pears and honey yoghurt. If you like, sprinkle with a little ground nutmeg or cinnamon.

nutritional count per serving 35.7g total fat (9.4g saturated fat); 3135kJ (750 cal); 81g carbohydrate; 21g protein; 12.6g fibre

tips Similarly to quinoa, amaranth is treated as a grain. You will be able to find the ingredients for this muesli either in the health food aisle at most supermarkets or health food stores. Store muesli in an airtight container in the fridge for up to 1 month.

STRAWBERRY & PASSIONFRUIT
BREAKFAST TRIFLE

PREP TIME 5 MINUTES **SERVES** 2

2 Weet-Bix (50g), broken into chunks

½ cup (40g) All-Bran cereal

1 cup (280g) low-fat plain yoghurt or soy yoghurt

⅓ cup (80ml) fresh passionfruit pulp

140g (4½ ounces) strawberries, sliced

1 Layer half each of the Weet-Bix and All-Bran in two 1¼-cup (310ml) glasses. Top with half each of the yoghurt, passionfruit and strawberries.
2 Repeat with remaining Weet-Bix, All-Bran and yoghurt. Top with remaining strawberries and passionfruit.

nutritional count per serving 2g total fat (0.5g saturated fat); 722kJ (172 cal); 36.1g carbohydrate; 16.2g protein; 15.5g fibre

tips Assemble the trifle just before you're ready to eat so the cereals keep their crunch. You will need about 4 passionfruit. You can make the trifle with any seasonal fruit combination or even with canned fruit in natural juices. Canned pears and frozen raspberries work well together.

QUINOA PORRIDGE

PREP + COOK TIME 20 MINUTES SERVES 2

½ cup (100g) white quinoa, rinsed

1½ cups (375ml) water

½ cup (125ml) skim milk or almond milk

1 medium red apple (150g), grated coarsely

⅓ cup (95g) plain yoghurt

1 tablespoon raw honey or pure maple syrup

1 medium mango (430g), sliced

1 tablespoon goji berries

2 tablespoons pistachios, roasted, chopped coarsely

1 Combine quinoa and the water in a small saucepan; bring to the boil. Reduce heat; simmer, covered, for 10 minutes. Add milk; cook, covered, for a further 5 minutes or until quinoa is tender. Stir in apple until combined.
2 Place yoghurt and honey in a small bowl; stir gently to swirl through.
3 Serve porridge topped with mango slices, goji berries, pistachios and honey yoghurt.

nutritional count per serving 9.3g total fat (2.4g saturated fat); 1923kJ (460 cal); 76.5g carbohydrate; 16g protein; 3.5g fibre

tips Although most quinoa comes rinsed, it's a good idea to rinse it yourself under cold water until the water runs clear. This removes any remaining outer coating, which has a bitter taste and can make it difficult to digest. Quinoa absorbs a lot of liquid, so depending on how you like your porridge, add a little boiling water at the end of step 1 to thin it out. We used a pink lady apple in this recipe.

MUSHROOM & PARMESAN
FRENCH TOAST

PREP + COOK TIME 15 MINUTES SERVES 2

2 eggs

½ cup (125ml) milk

2 teaspoons dijon mustard

¼ cup (20g) finely grated parmesan

4 x 2cm (¾-inch) thick slices sourdough bread

⅓ cup (80ml) olive oil

300g (9½ ounces) button mushrooms, sliced thinly

1 clove garlic, crushed

2 tablespoons fresh thyme leaves

2 teaspoons apple cider vinegar

10g (½ ounce) butter

¼ cup (60g) crème fraîche

¼ cup (20g) flaked parmesan

1 tablespoon finely chopped fresh chives

1 Using a fork, whisk eggs, milk, mustard and grated parmesan in a shallow dish until combined; season. Soak bread slices in egg mixture for 5 minutes, turning halfway through.

2 Meanwhile, heat 1½ tablespoons of the oil in a large frying pan over medium-high heat; cook half the mushrooms, without stirring, for 1 minute or until browned underneath. Cook, stirring, a further 2 minutes or until tender. Transfer to a heatproof dish; cover with foil. Repeat process with another 1½ tablespoons of the oil and remaining mushrooms, adding garlic and thyme during the last minute of cooking; stir in vinegar and half the butter. Combine all mushrooms in dish; cover to keep warm.

3 In same cleaned pan, heat remaining oil and remaining butter over medium heat; cook bread for 2 minutes each side or until golden.

4 Serve french toast topped with mushroom mixture, crème fraîche, flaked parmesan and chives.

nutritional count per serving 65.4g total fat (23.3g saturated fat); 3482kJ (833 cal); 32.8g carbohydrate; 27.7g protein; 4.4g fibre

FRUIT COMPOTES

PEAR, CARDAMOM & GINGER COMPOTE

PREP + COOK TIME 45 MINUTES SERVES 4

Place 4 (1kg) cored and thickly sliced packham pears in a medium saucepan with 1 cup water, 2 teaspoons freshly grated ginger, 6 bruised cardamom pods, 1 cinnamon stick and 1 tablespoon lemon juice; bring to the boil. Reduce heat; simmer, partially covered, 25 minutes, stirring occasionally, or until liquid has reduced slightly and pears are tender. Serve warm or chilled.

serving sugggestion Serve with vanilla yoghurt or muesli.

APPLE, RHUBARB & GOJI COMPOTE

PREP + COOK TIME 25 MINUTES SERVES 4

Place ½ cup fresh orange juice and 2 tablespoons rice malt syrup in a medium saucepan over low heat; cook, stirring, until syrup melts. Add 2 large (400g) coarsely chopped pink lady apples, 4cm (1½-inch) wide strip of orange rind, the seeds scraped from ½ vanilla bean and the pod; simmer, covered, for 5 minutes. Add 1 bunch (500g) trimmed, coarsely chopped rhubarb and 2 tablespoons goji berries; simmer gently, covered, for 10 minutes or until fruit is tender and still holding its shape. Serve warm or chilled.

serving sugggestion Serve with porridge or yoghurt. To turn into a dessert, add a crumble topping to make rhubarb and apple crumble.

VANILLA-ROASTED NECTARINES & PEACHES

PREP + COOK TIME 35 MINUTES SERVES 4

Preheat oven to 220°C/425°F. Grease a medium ovenproof dish with butter. Halve and remove stones from 3 medium (510g) yellow nectarines and 3 medium (450g) yellow peaches; place in dish. Split a vanilla bean lengthways, scrape seeds from halves, using the tip of a knife. Add vanilla bean and seeds to dish with 2 tablespoons pure maple syrup, 2 x 4cm (1½-inch) strips lemon rind, 1 tablespoon lemon juice and a pinch of sea salt flakes; turn fruit to coat. Arrange fruit in a single layer, cut-side up. Bake fruit for 20 minutes or until fruit is tender but still holds its shape. Serve warm or chilled.

serving sugggestion Serve with thick greek-style yoghurt, topped with nuts and seeds.

PLUM, RASPBERRY & ROSEMARY COMPOTE

PREP + COOK TIME 25 MINUTES SERVES 4

Halve and remove stones from 5 blood plums (450g); cut each half into thirds. Place plums in a large saucepan with ¼ cup water, 1 tablespoon lemon juice, 1 cinnamon stick and 2 sprigs rosemary; bring to the boil. Reduce heat; simmer, covered, for 5 minutes. Uncover; simmer, for a further 5 minutes or until plums are just tender. Stir in ½ cup raspberries and 2 teaspoons norbu (monk fruit sugar) or stevia granules until norbu dissolves. Remove from heat.

serving sugggestion Serve with thick greek-style yoghurt.

GREEN SMOOTHIE

PREP TIME 10 MINUTES
SERVES 2

You can use a variety of green vegetables or fruits, such as lettuce, pear or honeydew melon.

1 medium lime (90g)

1 medium apple (150g)

1 lebanese cucumber (130g)

½ medium avocado (125g)

320ml (10 ounces) canned coconut water

30g (1 ounce) baby spinach leaves

1 teaspoon finely grated fresh ginger

50g (1½ ounces) baby kale leaves

1 Remove rind with pith from lime; discard. Coarsely chop lime flesh, apple, cucumber and avocado.
2 Blend or process ingredients until smooth. Pour into two glasses; serve immediately.

nutritional count per serving 9.6g total fat (2.1g saturated fat); 768kJ (183 cal); 18.7g carbohydrate; 2.5g protein; 5.3g fibre

tips For smoothies it is best to use tender baby kale that way you won't need to remove the hard stems. If you like, top the smoothies with white or black chia seeds and toasted shredded coconut.

CHERRY & WALNUT SMOOTHIE

PREP TIME 15 MINUTES
(+ STANDING) SERVES 4

You need to start this recipe the day before.

½ cup (60g) walnuts

⅓ cup (55g) natural almonds

1¾ cups (430ml) water

750g (1½ pounds) frozen pitted cherries

2 teaspoons pure maple syrup

¼ cup (30g) walnuts, extra

1 tablespoon black chia seeds

1 Combine walnuts, almonds and the water in a medium bowl. Cover; stand overnight.
2 Blend nut mixture for 2 minutes or until as smooth as possible. Strain mixture through a muslin-lined sieve over a medium jug; twist and squeeze the cloth to extract as much liquid as possible. Discard solids in cloth.
3 Blend nut milk, cherries and syrup until smooth. Pour into 1-cup (250ml) glasses, top with extra walnuts and chia seeds. Serve immediately.

nutritional count per serving 20.5g total fat (1.3g saturated fat); 1422kJ (339 cal); 25.7g carbohydrate; 7.7g protein; 1.2g fibre

tips For a thicker smoothie, blend the chia seeds with the other smoothie ingredients. You can make other flavoured nut milks using 105g (3½ ounces) total of your favourite nuts and 1¾ cups (430ml) water. Use pecans instead of walnuts, if you like.

GREEN QUINOA
WITH SESAME EGGS

PREP + COOK TIME 25 MINUTES SERVES 2

½ cup (100g) white quinoa, rinsed

1 cup (250g) chicken or vegetable stock

4 eggs, at room temperature

2 teaspoons coconut oil

1 small clove garlic, crushed

1 fresh small red chilli, chopped finely

2 cups (80g) thinly sliced kale (see tip)

2 cups (90g) firmly packed thinly sliced silver beet (see tip)

1 tablespoon lemon juice

¼ cup finely chopped fresh flat-leaf parsley

1 tablespoon white sesame seeds

1 tablespoon black sesame seeds

1 teaspoon sea salt flakes

1 Place quinoa and stock in a medium saucepan; bring to the boil. Reduce heat to low-medium; simmer gently for 15 minutes or until most of the stock is absorbed. Remove from heat; cover, stand 5 minutes.

2 Meanwhile, cook eggs in a small saucepan of boiling water for 5 minutes. Remove immediately from pan; cool under cold running water for 30 seconds. Peel.

3 Heat coconut oil in a medium saucepan over medium heat, add garlic and chilli; cook stirring, for 2 minutes or until fragrant. Add kale and silver beet; stir until wilted. Stir in quinoa and juice; season to taste.

4 Combine parsley, sesame seeds and salt in a small bowl. Roll peeled eggs in parsley mixture.

5 Serve quinoa topped with eggs.

nutritional count per serving 23.8g total fat (8.6g saturated fat); 1957kJ (467cal); 35g carbohydrate; 25g protein; 7.6g fibre

tip You will need half a bunch of kale and half a bunch of silver beet for this recipe. Wash well before use.

BANANA &
CHOC-ALMOND TOASTIE

PREP + COOK TIME 15 MINUTES MAKES 2

4 square slices sourdough bread (180g) (see tips)

10g (½ ounce) butter, softened

2 tablespoons almond butter

1 teaspoon cacao powder

2 teaspoons rice malt syrup

1 medium banana (180g), sliced thinly

¼ teaspoon ground cinnamon

1 Preheat a jaffle or sandwich maker.

2 Spread one side of each bread slice with butter.

3 Stir almond butter, cacao and syrup in a small bowl until smooth.

4 Place two slices of bread buttered-side-down on a board; spread half the almond butter mixture on each slice, then top with banana, leaving a 1cm (½-inch) border. Top with remaining bread slices, buttered-side-up.

5 Cook sandwiches in jaffle maker for 5 minutes or until golden. Serve cut in half, dusted with cinnamon.

nutritional count per toastie 16.4g total fat (4.2g saturated fat); 2082kJ (498 cal); 69.6g carbohydrate; 16.3g protein; 4.6g fibre

tips You can use any bread you prefer – wholemeal, wholegrain and rye would all taste great, just make sure the slices are square to fit the jaffle maker. You can substitute any nut butter of your choice for the almond butter. Other great alternatives are coconut butter or ricotta, especially if you have a nut allergy.

SPELT & OAT SCONES
WITH BERRY CHIA SEED JAM

PREP + COOK TIME 50 MINUTES **SERVES** 8

This jam takes only 10 minutes to make. It won't store as long as regular jam, however it can be frozen in portions to extend the shelf life.

1 cup (150g) wholemeal plain (all-purpose) flour

1 cup (150g) white spelt flour

2 teaspoons baking powder

1 teaspoon fine sea salt flakes

100g (3 ounces) cold butter, chopped coarsely

¾ cup (180ml) buttermilk

1 tablespoon raw honey

1 tablespoon buttermilk, extra

2 tablespoons rolled oats

50g (1½ ounces) butter, extra

berry chia seed jam

400g (12½ ounces) frozen mixed berries

¼ cup (35g) white chia seeds

1 tablespoon pure maple syrup

1 teaspoon finely grated lemon rind

1 teaspoon lemon juice

1 vanilla bean, split lengthways, seeds scraped

1 Make berry chia seed jam.

2 Preheat oven to 220°C/425°F fan-forced (see tips). Line an oven tray with baking paper.

3 Sift flours, baking powder and salt into a large bowl; rub in butter until mixture resembles coarse breadcrumbs. Add buttermilk and honey. Using a dinner knife, cut liquid through mixture until it starts to clump. Turn out onto a floured surface; knead gently for 45 seconds or until dough just comes together. (Don't over work the dough or it will be tough.)

4 Shape dough into a 16cm (6½-inch) round on tray with floured hands. Mark the round into eight wedges, using the back of a floured knife. Brush top with extra buttermilk; sprinkle with oats.

5 Bake scones for 20 minutes or until top is golden. Serve warm with extra butter and jam.

berry chia seed jam Cook berries in a medium saucepan over medium heat, stirring occasionally, for 5 minutes or until berries release their juices. Reduce heat to low, add chia seeds and syrup; cook, stirring occasionally, for 6 minutes or until thickened slightly. Stir in rind, juice and vanilla seeds (keep vanilla pod for another use).

nutritional count per serving 18.7g total fat (10.7g saturated fat); 1475kJ (352 cal); 36g carbohydrate; 7g protein; 5.4g fibre

tips The even heat provided by the fan function of the oven will help give these scones an extra boost. For conventional ovens, increase the temperature by 10-20 degrees. Scones are best made on the day of serving. The jam can be made up to 3 days ahead; store in an airtight container in the fridge for up to 2 weeks or freeze for up to 1 month.

BREAKFAST SALAD WITH
POACHED EGGS & KALE PESTO

PREP + COOK TIME 25 MINUTES **SERVES** 2

¾ cup (45g) firmly packed baby leaves (see tips)

100g (3 ounces) brussels sprouts, shaved thinly

1 cup (150g) crunchy combo sprout mix

1 small carrot (80g), cut into matchsticks

2 tablespoons toasted sunflower seeds

2 tablespoons apple cider vinegar

1½ tablespoons avocado oil

1 teaspoon raw honey

1 tablespoon white vinegar

4 eggs

½ medium avocado (125g), sliced thinly

kale pesto

⅓ cup (55g) dry-roasted almonds

⅓ cup (50g) roasted cashews

2 small cloves garlic

2 cups (80g) baby kale, chopped coarsely

½ cup (125ml) extra virgin olive oil

1½ tablespoons apple cider vinegar

¼ cup (20g) finely grated parmesan

1 Make kale pesto.

2 Place baby leaves, brussels sprouts, sprout mix, carrot and seeds in a medium bowl; toss to combine. Whisk cider vinegar, 1 tablespoon of the oil and honey in a small bowl; season to taste. Add dressing to salad; toss to combine.

3 To poach eggs, half-fill a large, deep-frying pan with water, add white vinegar; bring to a gentle simmer. Break 1 egg into a cup. Using a wooden spoon, make a whirlpool in the water; slide egg into whirlpool. Repeat with 3 more eggs. Cook eggs for 3 minutes or until whites are set and the yolks are runny. Remove eggs with a slotted spoon; drain on a paper-towel-lined plate.

4 Divide salad between serving bowls; top with eggs and avocado. Spoon pesto on eggs; drizzle with remaining oil.

kale pesto Pulse nuts and garlic in a food processor until coarsely chopped. Add kale, oil and vinegar; pulse to a fine paste. Add parmesan, season with sea salt and cracked pepper; pulse until just combined. (Makes 1¼ cups)

nutritional count per serving 121.8g total fat (21.9g saturated fat); 5852kJ (1400 cal); 31.7g carbohydrate; 39.4g protein; 6.7g fibre

tips We used a baby leaf micro herb mix of sorrel, parsley, coriander (cilantro) and radish. Leftover pesto can be stored, covered with a light layer of oil, in an airtight container in the fridge for up to 1 week.

SEED CRACKERS
WITH SMASHED AVOCADO

PREP + COOK TIME 1 HOUR 30 MINUTES
SERVES 2 (MAKES 50 CRACKERS)

1 cup (200g) long-grain brown rice

2½ cups (625ml) water

1 cup (200g) tri-colour quinoa

2 cups (500ml) water, extra

¼ cup (g) sesame seeds

¼ cup (50g) linseeds (flaxseeds)

¼ cup (35g) chia seeds

¼ cup (35g) sunflower seeds

1 tablespoon finely chopped fresh lemon thyme

1 tablespoon finely chopped fresh oregano

1 tablespoon finely chopped fresh rosemary

1 teaspoon cracked black pepper

2 teaspoons onion powder

1 medium avocado (250g)

1 tablespoon lemon juice

2 teaspoons chia seeds, extra

45g (1½ ounces) snow pea shoots

pinch sumac, optional

1 Preheat oven 180°C/350°F.

2 Place brown rice and the water in a small saucepan; bring to the boil. Reduce heat to low; simmer, uncovered, for 25 minutes or until most of the water has evaporated. Remove from heat; stand, covered, for 10 minutes. Fluff with a fork, spread out over an oven tray; cool.

3 Place quinoa and the extra water in same pan; bring to the boil. Reduce heat to low; simmer, uncovered, for 10 minutes or until most of the water has evaporated. Remove from heat; stand, covered, for 10 minutes. Fluff with a fork, spread out over an oven tray; cool.

4 Process the rice with half the quinoa to a coarse paste; transfer to a large bowl. Add remaining quinoa, seeds, the herbs, pepper and onion powder, season; using your hands, combine well. Divide into four portions.

5 Line four oven trays with baking paper. Remove one of the pieces of baking paper. Flatten a portion of dough over paper, cover with plastic wrap then roll out with a rolling pin to 1mm-thick or as thin as possible. (Don't worry if there are holes, these will give the crackers texture and character.) Discard plastic; carefully lift the paper back onto the tray. Repeat with remaining portions of dough until you have four trays. Score the crackers into 5cm x 10cm (2-inch x 4-inch) lengths or triangles (or leave as whole sheets and break into pieces after baking).

6 Bake crackers for 20 minutes. Cover crackers with a sheet of baking paper and a second tray. Holding the hot tray with oven gloves, flip the crackers over onto the second tray; carefully remove lining paper. Repeat with remaining trays. Cook crackers for a further 20 minutes or until golden and crisp. Cool on trays.

7 To serve, roughly smash avocado with a fork in a small bowl with juice; season to taste. Place 4 crackers on each of two serving plates; top crackers with avocado mixture, extra chia seeds, snow pea shoots and sumac.

nutritional count per serving 26.5g total fat (4.9g saturated fat); 1597kJ (382 cal); 23.6g carbohydrate; 9g protein; 6.2g fibre

nutritional count per cracker (cracker only) 1.8g total fat (0.2g saturated fat); 192kJ (46 cal); 5.7g carbohydrate; 1.5g protein; 0.7g fibre

tips If the cracker mixture spreads past the paper when you're rolling it just cut those edges off. If you don't have enough oven trays, you can cook the crackers in two batches. Crackers can be stored in an airtight container for up to 1 month.

SEEDAHOLIC BREAD
WITH ALMOND BUTTER & PEAR

PREP + COOK TIME 2 HOURS 30 MINUTES (+ STANDING & COOLING) SERVES 2 (MAKES 10 SLICES)

1½ cups (135g) rolled oats

1½ cups (120g) quinoa flakes

1 cup (150g) sunflower seeds

1 cup (200g) pepitas (pumpkin seeds)

⅔ cup (130g) flax seeds

½ cup (70g) white chia seeds

½ cup (80g) chopped almond kernels

½ cup (70g) chopped hazelnuts

½ cup (40g) psyllium husks

2 teaspoons sea salt flakes

3½ cups (875ml) warm water

2 tablespoons raw honey

⅔ cup (140g) coconut oil, melted

¼ cup (65g) almond butter

1 medium packham pear (250g), sliced thinly

1 tablespoon olive oil

1 Grease a 1.5-litre (6-cup), 14cm x 24cm (5½-inch x 9½-inch) loaf pan; line the base and two long sides with baking paper, extending the paper over the edge.

2 Place dry ingredients in a large bowl. Place the water, honey and coconut oil in a large jug; stir until dissolved. Pour over dry ingredients; stir to combine. (The mixture will be firm, if it is too stiff add extra tablespoons of water, one at a time.)

3 Spoon seed mixture into pan; shape with your hands into a loaf shape. Cover surface with plastic wrap; stand at room temperature for 2 hours to allow ingredients to absorb the liquid and set the bread into shape.

4 Preheat oven 200°C/400°F.

5 Bake bread for 30 minutes. Invert bread onto a wire rack on an oven tray; peel away lining paper. Return bread to oven on tray; bake a further 1 hour 20 minutes (see tips) or until a skewer inserted into the centre comes out clean. Leave for 3 hours or until completely cool before slicing.

6 To serve, spread 4 slices of seedaholic bread with almond butter, top with pear slices; drizzle with olive oil. Divide between two serving plates. Season to taste.

nutritional count per serving 122.8g total fat (37.2g saturated fat); 6726kJ (1609 cal); 77.2g carbohydrate; 44.8g protein; 18.3g fibre

nutritional count per slice (bread only) 48.7g total fat (16.9g saturated fat); 2646kJ (633 cal); 28.6g carbohydrate; 18.7g protein; 7.3g fibre

tips Psyllium husks are available from vitamin and health food stores. Position the shelf in the oven so the top of the bread sits in the middle of the oven. If the bread starts to overbrown during baking, cover it loosely with foil. Bread will keep in an airtight container in the fridge for up to 2 weeks. Freeze individual slices in zip-top bags for up to 1 month.

SWEET POTATO RÖSTI
DUKKAH BRUNCH

PREP + COOK TIME 30 MINUTES SERVES 2

240g (7½ ounces) purple-skinned white-flesh sweet potato, peeled, grated coarsely

1 medium onion (150g), grated coarsely

1 egg white

⅓ cup (25g) finely grated parmesan

1 tablespoon finely chopped fresh flat-leaf parsley

1 tablespoon finely chopped fresh dill

1 clove garlic, crushed

2 tablespoons olive oil

20g (¾ ounce) butter

1 tablespoon white vinegar

4 eggs

150g (4½ ounces) hot-smoked salmon, flaked

¼ cup (70g) greek-style yoghurt

2 teaspoons dukkah

2 tablespoons fresh coriander (cilantro) leaves

lemon wedges, to serve

1 Preheat oven to 180°C/350°F. Line an oven tray with baking paper.

2 Combine sweet potato and onion in a medium bowl; squeeze out excess liquid, return vegetables to bowl. Stir in egg white, parmesan, herbs and garlic; season.

3 Heat half the oil and half the butter in a large frying pan over medium heat; spoon half the sweet potato mixture into pan, flatten to a 10cm (4-inch) round. Cook for 3 minutes each side or until golden. Drain on paper towel; place on tray, season with salt. Repeat with remaining oil, butter and sweet potato mixture to make two rösti in total.

4 Bake rösti 10 minutes or until crisp and cooked through.

5 Meanwhile, to poach eggs, half-filll a large, deep-frying pan wth water, add white vinegar; bring to a gentle simmer. Break 1 egg into a cup. Using a wooden spoon, make a whirlpool in the water; slide egg into whirlpool. Repeat with 3 more eggs. Cook eggs for 3 minutes or until whites are set and the yolks are runny. Remove eggs with a slotted spoon; drain on a paper-towel-lined plate.

6 Divide rösti between plates; top with salmon, eggs and yoghurt. Sprinkle with dukkah and coriander, serve with lemon wedges.

nutritional count per serving 46g total fat (16g saturated fat); 3055kJ (730 cal); 32g carbohydrate; 44g protein; 5g fibre

tips Dukkah is a Middle Eastern nut and spice mixture available from supermarkets and delis. You can substitute kumara (orange sweet potato) or potato for the white sweet potato in the rösti and hot-smoked trout or white fish for the salmon.

ELECTROLYTE BOOSTER

PREP TIME 10 MINUTES MAKES 1 LITRE

Blend 2 cups coconut water, 400g (12½ ounces) frozen pineapple, 1 small (200g) avocado, ½ trimmed, chopped baby (65g) fennel, ½ cup fresh mint leaves, 2 cups firmly packed baby spinach and 2 tablespoons lime juice in a high-speed blender until smooth. Serve over ice.

tip Frozen pineapple is available from supermarkets or you can freeze your own portioned, peeled, cored and chopped pineapple in zip-top bags.

JUST LIKE A CHOCOLATE THICK SHAKE...

PREP TIME 10 MINUTES MAKES 1 LITRE

Blend 2 cups unsweetened almond milk, 2 ripe medium (260g) chopped frozen bananas, 1 small (200g) chopped avocado, 1 cup firmly packed baby spinach, 2 tablespoons cacao powder, ⅓ cup vanilla bean whey protein powder (optional) or yoghurt and 1 tablespoon raw honey in a high-speed blender until smooth. Serve over ice, dusted with ¼ teaspoon extra cacao powder.

BERRY BERRY LUSCIOUS

PREP TIME 10 MINUTES MAKES 3 CUPS

Soak 2 tablespoons of goji berries in 1 cup chilled coconut milk blend (see tip) for 10 minutes in a small bowl. Transfer to a high-speed blender; add 2 cups frozen mixed berries, 1 cup firmly packed baby spinach and another cup chilled coconut milk blend. Blend until smooth. Serve over ice, topped with 1 tablespoon each goji berries and mixed berries.

tip We used Pureharvest Coco Quench a blend of coconut and rice milks; it has a thinner consistency than canned coconut milk, but still has a great coconut milk taste.

GREEN TEA & KIWI SIPPER

**PREP TIME 10 MINUTES (+ COOLING)
MAKES 1 LITRE**

Brew 2 green tea bags in 2 cups boiling water for 5 minutes. Discard tea bags. Stir in 1 tablespoon raw honey. Cool in the refrigerator. Place cooled tea in a high-speed blender with 1 cup frozen green grapes, 2 medium (170g) peeled chopped kiwifruits, 1 cup fresh mint leaves and 1 cup firmly packed baby spinach until smooth. Serve immediately over ice.

tip This drink separates quickly, so it is best made just before serving.

DRINKS

QUINOA & PEAR BIRCHER
WITH COCONUT FRUIT SALAD

PREP + COOK TIME *10 MINUTES* **SERVES** 2

You can use grated apple or nashi instead of the pear.

1 tablespoon pepitas (pumpkin seeds)

1 tablespoon sunflower seeds

1 medium pear (230g), grated coarsely

1½ cups (120g) quinoa flakes

½ cup (125ml) coconut milk

½ cup (125ml) unsweetened apple juice

coconut fruit salad

1 medium young drinking coconut (900g)

50g (1½ ounces) raspberries

60g (2 ounces) blueberries

1 tablespoon long thin strips of orange rind

1 medium orange (240g), peeled, segmented (see tips)

1 Make coconut fruit salad.

2 Stir pepitas and sunflower seeds in a small frying pan over medium heat for 2 minutes or until toasted.

3 Combine pear, quinoa, coconut milk, apple juice and reserved coconut water (from coconut fruit salad) in a medium bowl.

4 Divide bircher between two serving bowls; spoon fruit salad on top. Sprinkle with toasted seeds.

coconut fruit salad Insert the tip of a small knife into the soft spot on the base of the coconut, using a twisting action. Place coconut over a glass; drain coconut water. Reserve ½ cup (125ml) for bircher. Wrap coconut in a clean towel, break open with a hammer, or by smashing it onto the floor. Spoon out the soft coconut flesh; slice into thin strips. Combine coconut flesh with remaining ingredients in a small bowl. Cover; refrigerate until required.

nutritional count per serving 26.1g total fat (16.1g saturated fat); 2508kJ (600 cal); 70g carbohydrate; 14.5g protein; 9.9g fibre

tips To segment an orange, cut off the rind with the white pith, following the curve of the fruit. Cut down either side of each segment close to the membrane to release the segment. Young drinking coconuts are available from green grocers and some supermarkets. Look for a freshly squeezed apple juice from single variety apples such as granny smith, as they will have a clean fresh sweet and tart taste. Store bircher in an airtight container in the refrigerator for up to 4 days.

BANANA PANCAKES WITH
LABNE & BLUEBERRY COMPOTE

PREP + COOK TIME 40 MINUTES (+ STANDING) **SERVES** 4

You will need to start the labne 2 days ahead, otherwise serve the pancakes with greek-style yoghurt.

1 medium ripe banana (200g)

¼ cup (35g) coconut flour

¼ teaspoon bicarbonate of soda (baking soda)

¼ teaspoon ground cinnamon

2 eggs

1 vanilla bean, split lengthways, seeds scraped

½ cup (125ml) unsweetened almond milk

2 tablespoons coconut oil

1 medium banana (200g), extra, sliced thickly

2 tablespoons roasted coconut chips

labne

500g (1 pound) greek-style yoghurt

½ teaspoon sea salt

1 teaspoon finely grated lemon rind

blueberry compote

1 cup (250ml) apple juice

½ cup (75g) coconut sugar

2 cups (280g) frozen blueberries

1 Make labne.

2 Make blueberry compote.

3 Mash banana to a paste in a medium bowl with a fork. Add coconut flour, soda, cinnamon, eggs, vanilla seeds and almond milk; stir to combine.

4 Melt one-third of the coconut oil in a large non-stick frying pan over low-medium heat. Spoon tablespoons of batter into pan, flatten slightly; cook for 2 minutes or until bubbles appear on the surface. Using two spatulas, as mixture is delicate, carefully turn over; cook a further 1 minute or until cooked through. Remove from pan; keep warm. Repeat two more times with remaining coconut oil and batter to make 12 pancakes in total.

5 Serve pancakes topped with labne, sliced banana, coconut chips and blueberry compote.

labne Line a sieve with two layers of muslin (or a clean Chux cloth); place it over a bowl. Stir ingredients together in a small bowl; spoon into the lined sieve. Tie the cloth close to the surface of the yoghurt; refrigerate for 48 hours. (Makes 260g/8½ ounces)

blueberry compote Stir juice and coconut sugar in a medium saucepan over low heat until sugar dissolves. Bring to a simmer; cook for 10 minutes or until reduced to a thin syrup. Add frozen blueberries; stir gently until berries are coated and thawed.

nutritional count per serving 24.3g total fat (15.8g saturated fat); 2337kJ (559 cal); 69.2g carbohydrate; 14.3g protein; 3.5g fibre

BAKED TURKISH EGGS
WITH LAMB MINCE

PREP + COOK TIME 25 MINUTES   SERVES 2

¼ cup (60ml) extra virgin olive oil

1 medium onion (150g), chopped finely

2 cloves garlic, crushed

½ teaspoon ground mixed spice

½ teaspoon ground cinnamon

¼ teaspoon chilli flakes

150g (4½ ounces) minced (ground) lamb

1 large tomato (220g), chopped coarsely

2 tablespoons lemon juice

½ teaspoon stevia granules or norbu (monk fruit sugar)

1 tablespoon finely chopped fresh mint

1 tablespoon finely chopped fresh flat-leaf parsley

4 eggs

¼ cup loosely packed fresh micro mint leaves

¼ cup loosely packed fresh flat-leaf parsley leaves, extra

2 lebanese flatbreads (230g), quartered

cucumber yoghurt

½ lebanese cucumber (130g)

½ cup (95g) greek-style yoghurt

1 clove garlic, crushed

1 teaspoon finely grated lemon rind

1 Make cucumber yoghurt.

2 Heat 2 tablespoons of the oil in a large frying pan over medium heat; cook onion, garlic, spices and chilli flakes, for 3 minutes or until soft. Add mince; cook, breaking mince up with a wooden spoon, for 5 minutes or until browned. Add tomato, juice and stevia; cook, for 2 minutes. Remove from heat; stir in chopped herbs. Season to taste.

3 Make four indents in mince mixture with the back of a spoon. Carefully crack eggs into indents; season eggs. Cook, covered, over medium heat for a further 6 minutes or until whites of eggs have set but yolks are still runny.

4 Drizzle with remaining oil; top with cucumber yoghurt, micro mint and extra parsley. Serve with flatbread.

cucumber yoghurt Coarsely grate cucumber; squeeze out excess water. Combine cucumber with remaining ingredients in a small bowl; season to taste.

nutritional count per serving 51.9g total fat (14g saturated fat); 4197kJ (1004 cal); 79.6g carbohydrate; 49.4g protein; 4.6g fibre

tips This is a great dish for a group, just multiply the recipe. You can use minced beef, pork or chicken instead of the lamb, if you like.

SUPER SEED BOWL
WITH APPLE & YOGHURT

PREP + COOK TIME 10 MINUTES SERVES 2

2 medium green apples (300g), cut into matchsticks

2 tablespoons lemon juice

½ cup (125ml) coconut water

100g (3 ounces) strawberries, sliced thickly

½ cup (140g) greek-style yoghurt

2 tablespoons raw honey

super seed mix

2 tablespoons sunflower seeds

2 tablespoons pepitas (pumpkin seeds)

1½ tablespoons sesame seeds

1½ tablespoons poppy seeds

1½ tablespoons chia seeds

1½ tablespoons linseeds (flaxseeds)

2 tablespoons currants

2 tablespoons goji berries

1 Make super seed mix.

2 Combine apple and juice in a medium bowl.

3 Divide apple mixture and half the seed mix between two bowls, add coconut water. Top with strawberries and yoghurt; drizzle with honey and sprinkle with remaining seed mix.

super seed mix Stir sunflower seeds and pepitas in a small frying pan over medium heat for 2 minutes or until lightly golden. Add sesame seeds, poppy seeds, chia seeds and linseeds; stir for 30 seconds or until all are toasted. Remove from pan; cool. Stir in currants and goji berries. (Makes 1 cup)

nutritional count per serving 31.2g total fat (6.2g saturated fat); 2596kJ (621 cal); 65.9g carbohydrate; 18.1g protein; 9.4g fibre

tips When in season, you can use pears instead of apples. Super seed mix can be made ahead. Store seed mix in an airtight container or jar in the fridge for up to 3 months.

VEGIE & EGG
POWER STACK

PREP + COOK TIME 40 MINUTES SERVES 4

400g (12½ ounces) medium kumara (orange sweet potato) (see tips)

8 fresh shiitake mushrooms (140g), stems trimmed

¼ cup (60ml) olive oil

2 teaspoons chopped fresh rosemary

1 long fresh red chilli, seeded, chopped

2 tablespoons sunflower seeds

2 cups (80g) baby kale

¼ cup (20g) finely grated parmesan

1 tablespoon white vinegar

8 fresh eggs

3 green heirloom tomatoes (380g), sliced (see tips)

4 baby target beetroot (beets) (80g), sliced thinly (see tips)

½ cup baby micro cress

lemon aïoli

1 egg yolk

1 small clove garlic, chopped

1 tablespoon finely grated lemon rind

1 teaspoon fresh chopped rosemary

2 tablespoons lemon juice

½ teaspoon raw honey

½ cup (125ml) olive oil

1 Preheat oven to 200°C/400°F. Line an oven tray with baking paper.

2 Cut kumara into eight 5mm (¼-inch) thick rounds. Place on tray with mushrooms, 2 tablespoons of the oil, rosemary and chilli; toss to coat. Bake for 25 minutes or until kumara is tender.

3 Meanwhile, make lemon aïoli.

4 Heat remaining oil in a medium frying pan over medium heat; cook sunflower seeds, stirring, for 2 minutes or until toasted. Stir in kale, turn off heat; leave for the residual heat to wilt leaves. Add parmesan; season to taste.

5 To poach eggs, half-fill a large, deep-frying pan with water, add vinegar; bring to a gentle simmer. Break 1 egg into a cup. Using a wooden spoon, make a whirlpool in the water; slide egg into whirlpool. Repeat with 3 more eggs. Cook eggs for 3 minutes or until whites are set and the yolks are runny. Remove eggs with a slotted spoon; drain on a paper-towel-lined plate. Keep warm. Repeat poaching with remaining eggs.

6 Spoon 2 tablespoons of the aïoli onto each plate. Build two stacks on each plate with kumara, tomato, mushrooms then kale mixture. Top each stack with a poached egg, sliced beetroot and micro cress.

lemon aïoli Process egg yolk, garlic, rind, rosemary, juice and honey in a small food processor for 1 minute. With motor operating, gradually add oil, drop by drop at first, then in a slow steady stream until mixture is thick and emulsified. Season to taste. (Makes ⅔ cup)

nutritional count per serving 56g total fat (11g saturated fat); 2969kJ (709 cal); 27g carbohydrate; 22.5g protein; 6.6g fibre

tips Try to buy a kumara with a diameter of 7cm (2¾ inches) as it will provide the base for your stack, and tomatoes of a similar size. If heirloom green tomatoes are hard to find, use red. Target beetroots are available from specialist green grocers and grower's markets. If they're unavailable, use radishes or a little shaved fennel instead.

HORCHATA
PORRIDGE SHAKE

PREP + COOK TIME 15 MINUTES (+ REFRIGERATION)
SERVES 4 (MAKES 1 LITRE)

You will need to start the recipe the night before. This recipe is perfect for a breakfast on the go, simply pour into a bottle, jar or jug with a lid and away you go.

1 vanilla bean

1 litre (4 cups) unsweetened almond milk

1 cup (90g) rolled oats

1 tablespoon raw honey

½ teaspoon sea salt

1 tablespoon rolled oats, extra

⅓ cup (24g) flaked almonds

½ teaspoon ground cinnamon

1 Split vanilla beans in half lengthways; using the tip of a small knife, scrape out seeds. Combine vanilla seeds and pod with almond milk, oats and honey in a medium jug. Cover; refrigerate overnight.

2 Preheat oven to 180°C/350°F. Place extra oats on an oven tray; roast for 5 minutes. Add almonds; roast for another 5 minutes or until lightly golden.

3 Discard vanilla bean from milk mixture. Blend or process milk mixture until smooth; stir in salt.

4 Pour shake into four glasses, top with roasted almond mixture; sprinkle with cinnamon. Serve immediately.

nutritional count per serving 8.7g total fat (0.6g saturated fat); 829kJ (198 cal); 27g carbohydrate; 8.6g protein; 3.5g fibre

tip For a quick version, leave out the oats (and the overnight refrigeration); blend chilled milk, vanilla seeds, honey and salt together. Serve immediately.

GRAIN-FREE COCONUT & VANILLA MUESLI

PREP + COOK TIME 30 MINUTES (+ COOLING)
SERVES 4 (MAKES 4¾ CUPS)

2 vanilla beans

2½ cups (125g) flaked coconut

½ cup (80g) natural almonds, chopped coarsely

½ cup (80g) brazil nuts, chopped coarsely

½ cup (60g) pecans, chopped coarsely

¼ cup (35g) sunflower seeds

½ cup (100g) virgin coconut oil, melted

2 tablespoons raw honey

½ teaspoon sea salt

1 Preheat oven to 160°C/300°F. Grease and line two large oven trays with baking paper.

2 Split vanilla beans in half lengthways; using the tip of a small knife, scrape out seeds. Place seeds and pods in a large bowl with remaining ingredients; stir to combine. Spread mixture evenly between trays.

3 Bake muesli for 20 minutes, stirring occasionally to break into clumps, or until lightly golden. Cool.

nutritional count per serving 88.8g total fat (49g saturated fat); 3916kJ (935 cal); 21.5g carbohydrate; 12.6g protein; 5.6g fibre

tip Store muesli in an airtight container in the fridge for up to 4 weeks.

serving suggestion Serve with milk or yoghurt.

STRAWBERRY & ALMOND
SWEET FRITTATA

PREP + COOK TIME 30 MINUTES SERVES 4

250g (8 ounces) strawberries, hulled

1 tablespoon coconut sugar

1 vanilla bean

6 eggs

2 tablespoons coconut sugar, extra

⅓ cup (40g) ground almonds

10g (½ ounce) butter

100g (3 ounces) firm ricotta, crumbled coarsely

⅓ cup (55g) dry-roasted almonds, chopped coarsely

1 Thinly slice half the strawberries; cut remaining strawberries in half. Combine halved strawberries with coconut sugar in a small bowl. Reserve sliced strawberries.

2 Split vanilla bean lengthways; using the tip of a knife, scrape the seeds. Reserve pod for another use (see tips).

3 Place vanilla seeds, eggs, extra coconut sugar and ground almonds in a medium bowl; whisk until combined.

4 Preheat grill (broiler) to high.

5 Melt butter in a 24cm (9½-inch) non-stick ovenproof frying pan over medium heat. Add egg mixture, top with sliced strawberries, ricotta and half the chopped almonds. Reduce heat to low; cook, for 8 minutes or until half set. Place pan under grill for a further 8 minutes or until ricotta is lightly browned and mixture just set.

6 Serve immediately topped with halved strawberries and remaining chopped almonds. Drizzle with some honey and sprinkle with black chia seeds, if you like.

nutritional count per serving 24.3g total fat (5.9g saturated fat); 1438kJ (344 cal); 12.5g carbohydrate; 18g protein; 1.8g fibre

tips The unused vanilla pod can be wrapped and frozen for up to 1 year. Use in recipes where a vanilla bean is called for. You can use macadamias and hazelnuts instead of the almonds, if you like.

LUNCH or DINNER

QUINOA, KALE &
FETTA PATTIES

PREP + COOK TIME 1 HOUR
(+ STANDING & REFRIGERATION) SERVES 6

*Prepared relishes and chutneys contain vast amounts
of sugar so there is good reason to make your own.
Our quick version uses the natural sweetness of beetroot.*

¾ cup (150g) quinoa, rinsed

1¼ cups (310ml) water

1 small zucchini (90g), grated coarsely

1 teaspoon fine sea salt

120g (4 ounces) fetta, crumbled coarsely

¾ cup (80g) parmesan, grated finely

3 eggs, beaten lightly

1 cup (35g) loosely packed shredded curly kale

⅓ cup coarsely chopped fresh flat-leaf parsley

½ cup (35g) day-old sourdough breadcrumbs

1 clove garlic, crushed

2 teaspoons finely grated lemon rind

¼ cup (60ml) olive oil

4 wholegrain barley wraps (180g)

½ cup (140g) greek-style yoghurt

1 medium lemon (140g), cut into wedges

beetroot relish

1 teaspoon cumin seeds

1 medium beetroot (beet) (175g),
cut into thin matchsticks

¼ cup (60ml) sherry vinegar

½ medium red onion (75g), sliced thinly

2 tablespoons extra virgin olive oil

1 tablespoon fresh thyme leaves

1 Place quinoa and the water in a small saucepan over
medium heat; bring to the boil. Reduce heat to low;
cook, covered, for 15 minutes or until water is absorbed.
Remove from heat; stand covered, for 10 minutes.
Spread over a tray; cool.
2 Combine zucchini and salt in a small sieve over a
small bowl; stand for 30 minutes.
3 Meanwhile, make beetroot relish.
4 Squeeze zucchini to remove excess liquid. Combine
zucchini, quinoa, fetta, parmesan, egg, kale, parsley,
breadcrumbs, garlic and rind in a medium bowl; season.
Cover; refrigerate for 1 hour.
5 Preheat oven to 160°C/325°F. Line an oven tray with
baking paper.
6 Shape firmly packed ⅓-cup of mixture with wet hands into
patties; place on tray. Cover; refrigerate for 1 hour to firm.
7 Heat half the oil in a large frying pan over medium heat;
cook half the patties, for 3 minutes each side or until golden
and cooked through. (Take care turning the patties as the
mixture is quite delicate.) Transfer to the oven tray; keep
warm in the oven. Repeat with remaining oil and patties.
8 Serve quinoa patties with beetroot relish, wraps, yoghurt
and lemon wedges.

beetroot relish Stir cumin seeds in a small frying pan over
medium heat for 30 seconds or until fragrant and toasted.
Pound seeds in a mortar and pestle until coarsely crushed.
Transfer to a medium bowl; stir in remaining ingredients
until combined. Season to taste.

nutritional count per serving 30.5g total fat (10g saturated
fat); 2128kJ (509 cal); 32g carbohydrate; 21.2g protein;
3.5g fibre

tip Patties can be made up to 2 days ahead; cover and
refrigerate until required.

FENNEL, APPLE &
PISTACHIO CHICKEN SALAD

PREP + COOK TIME 25 MINUTES (+ COOLING) SERVES 4

When poaching chicken, it is easy to overcook it and make it tough. The secret to keeping it tender and moist, is to finish off the cooking in the gentle residual heat of the pan. This method also works well when you are cooking fish.

2 cups (500ml) chicken stock

2 cups (500ml) water

4 thin slices lemon

4 cloves garlic, bruised (see tip)

6 fresh thyme sprigs

2 x 200g (6½-ounce) free-range chicken breasts

½ cup (125ml) lemon juice

1 tablespoon dijon mustard

⅓ cup (80ml) extra virgin olive oil

1 small fennel (130g), sliced thinly

1 medium apple (150g), sliced thinly

1 cup (40g) trimmed watercress

1 cup firmly packed fresh flat-leaf parsley leaves

1 cup firmly packed torn fresh mint

1 medium avocado (250g), sliced thinly

½ cup (60g) pistachios, chopped coarsely

1 Place stock, the water, lemon slices, garlic and thyme in a medium saucepan over medium heat. Add chicken; bring to the boil. Reduce heat; simmer for 4 minutes. Cover pan, turn off heat; set aside to cool to room temperature. Remove chicken; shred coarsely. (Reserve poaching liquid for another use; see tips.)

2 Whisk juice and mustard in a small bowl until combined; gradually whisk in oil until combined. Season to taste.

3 Combine fennel, apple, watercress, herbs and avocado in a large bowl. Add chicken and dressing; toss to combine. Season to taste. Serve salad topped with pistachios.

nutritional count per serving 41.7g total fat (7.7g saturated fat); 2268kJ (542 cal); 11g carbohydrate; 28g protein; 7.2g fibre

tips To bruise garlic, place the flat side of a cook's knife on the unpeeled clove; using the heel of your other hand push down on the knife to flatten it. Remove the skin. Store the reserved poaching liquid in the refrigerator for up to 3 days.

HONEY-ROASTED HAINANESE
CHICKEN RICE BANQUET

PREP + COOK TIME 2 HOURS **(+ REFRIGERATION) SERVES** 6

You will need to start this recipe the day before.

1.6kg (3¼-pound) whole chicken

2 tablespoons rock salt

2 green onions (scallions), cut into 5cm (2-inch) lengths

50g (1½-ounce) piece ginger, sliced

2 tablespoons raw honey

2 teaspoons chinese five spice

¼ teaspoon ground white pepper

2 tablespoons rice wine vinegar

2 tablespoons light soy sauce

1 lebanese cucumber (130g)

1 tablespoon rice wine vinegar, extra

1 cup loosely packed coriander (cilantro) sprigs

sliced fresh long red chilli and extra soy sauce, to serve

broth

1 litre (4 cups) chicken stock

1 litre (4 cups) water

300g (9½ ounces) daikon, chopped finely

2 green onions (scallions), cut into 5cm (2-inch) lengths

50g (1½-ounce) piece ginger, sliced

rice

2 cups (400g) medium-grain brown rice

1 litre (4 cups) chicken stock

15g (½-ounce) piece ginger, sliced

2 cloves garlic, unpeeled, bruised

chilli ginger sauce

2 fresh long red chillies, chopped coarsely

3 large cloves garlic, chopped

50g (1½-ounce) piece ginger, peeled, chopped

1 green onion (scallion), chopped *(continued next column)*

2 tablespoons dark soy sauce

1 teaspoon raw honey

1 Cut off chicken wings using poultry shears or a sharp knife and pull off any excess fat from chicken cavity; reserve trimmings for rice. Rub chicken with salt; rinse in cold water, pat dry with paper towel. Pull chicken thighs away from body; gently massage chicken flesh.
2 Fill chicken cavity with green onion and ginger; secure legs with kitchen string. Whisk honey, five spice, pepper, vinegar and sauce in a large bowl, add chicken; turn to coat. Leave, breast-side down, in marinade. Cover; refrigerate, overnight, turning occasionally.
3 Remove chicken from fridge; bring to room temperature. Preheat oven to 240°C/475°F.
4 Meanwhile, place broth ingredients in a medium saucepan; season. Bring to the boil. Reduce heat; simmer 30 minutes, skimming foam off during cooking.
5 Roast chicken 20 minutes. Reduce oven to 200°C/400°F; roast a further 30 minutes, basting occasionally with remaining marinade, or until juices run clear when the thickest part of a thigh is pierced. Cover; keep warm.
6 Meanwhile, make rice.
7 Process chilli ginger sauce ingredients until smooth.
8 Using a julienne peeler or spiraliser, cut cucumber into 'spaghetti'; combine with extra vinegar in a small bowl.
9 Cut chicken into six pieces. Place rice in serving bowls, top with chicken and cucumber 'spaghetti'. Spoon broth over rice and pan juices over chicken; top with coriander. Serve with chilli ginger sauce, sliced chilli and extra soy.

rice Cook reserved chicken trimmings in a saucepan over medium heat until fat is rendered; discard solids. Stir in rice to coat. Add stock, ginger and garlic; bring to the boil. Reduce heat to low; cook, covered, 45 minutes or liquid is absorbed.

nutritional count per serving 19.4g total fat (5.5g saturated fat); 2537kJ (606 cal); 69g carbohydrate; 36.6g protein; 5g fibre

SEEDED CAULIFLOWER
FALAFEL

PREP + COOK TIME 1 HOUR SERVES 6 (MAKES 30 FALAFEL)

½ cup (100g) pepitas (pumpkin seeds)

½ cup (75g) sunflower seeds

¼ cup (35g) sesame seeds

2 tablespoons linseeds (flaxseeds)

700g (1½ pounds) cauliflower, cut into florets

2 cloves garlic, crushed

1½ tablespoons cumin seeds, crushed

1½ tablespoons coriander seeds, crushed

½ cup loosely packed fresh mint leaves

½ cup loosely packed fresh flat-leaf parsley leaves

½ cup (140g) tahini

2 tablespoons psyllium husks (see tips)

2 tablespoons lemon juice

¼ cup (60ml) water

rice bran oil, for deep-frying

salad

1 small red onion (100g), sliced thinly into rings

250g (8 ounces) grape tomatoes, sliced crossways

¼ cup (60ml) red wine vinegar

140g (4½ ounces) persian fetta

hummus

400g (12½ ounces) canned chickpeas (garbanzo beans), undrained

¼ cup (70g) tahini

1 clove garlic

1½ tablespoons lemon juice

1 teaspoon cumin seeds, crushed

1 Make salad and hummus.

2 Heat a medium frying pan over medium-high heat, add pepitas, sunflower seeds, sesame seeds and linseeds; cook, stirring, for 2 minutes or until sesame seeds are golden.

3 Process toasted seeds with cauliflower and remaining ingredients (except rice bran oil) to a coarse paste; season well. Line an oven tray with baking paper. Using a dessert spoon, scoop up a mound of mixture. Hold a second dessert spoon the same size upside down and drag it over the falafel mixture in an arc shape as you reach the other side, bring the top of the spoon under the scoop of falafel mixture transferring it onto it in the process. Using the first spoon, push the quenelle-shaped falafel onto the tray.

4 Fill a medium saucepan two-thirds full with oil, heat to 160°C/325°F (or until oil sizzles when a small cube of bread is added). Fry, six falafel at a time, for 5 minutes or until dark golden and cooked through. Drain on paper towel.

5 Spoon hummus onto plates, top with falafel and salad. If you like, sprinkle with extra mint and parsley leaves.

salad Place onion, tomato and vinegar in a small bowl; stand for 30 minutes. Stir in fetta.

hummus Process chickpeas and canning liquid with remaining ingredients for 3 minutes or until smooth.

nutritional count per serving 50.7g total fat (9.5g saturated fat); 2629kJ (629 cal); 15.8g carbohydrate; 23.1g protein; 12.6g fibre

tips Psyllium husks are obtained from the seeds of a plant native to India. They are useful for their binding qualities and are a good source of dietary fibre. Buy at vitamin and health food shops. Crushing whole spices in a pestle and mortar yourself adds a greater depth of flavour than you'd get from using the ready ground version of the same spice.

ZUCCHINI & RICOTTA FRITTERS
WITH CARROT RELISH

PREP + COOK TIME 40 MINUTES SERVES 4

600g (1¼ pounds) zucchini, grated coarsely

1 tablespoon sea salt flakes

2 cloves garlic, crushed

2 green onions (scallions), chopped finely

2 tablespoons coarsely chopped fresh mint

2 eggs

2 teaspoons finely grated lemon rind

¾ cup (90g) ground almonds

½ cup (120g) firm ricotta

¼ cup (60ml) olive oil

100g (3 ounces) baby rocket (arugula)

carrot relish

2 tablespoons olive oil

2 cloves garlic, crushed

¼ teaspoon chilli flakes

3 medium carrots (360g), cut into thin matchsticks

¼ cup (40g) currants

2 tablespoons norbu (monk fruit sugar)

¼ cup (60ml) red wine vinegar

½ cup (125ml) water

1 teaspoon ground cardamom

400g (12½ ounces) vine-ripened tomatoes, seeded, chopped coarsely

1 Combine zucchini and salt in a medium bowl. Stand for 15 minutes.
2 Meanwhile, make carrot relish.
3 Squeeze excess liquid from zucchini. Combine zucchini with garlic, green onion, mint, eggs, rind, ground almonds and ricotta in a medium bowl; season.
4 Heat half the oil in a large frying pan over medium heat. Pour heaped ¼-cups fritter mixture into pan; cook for 3 minutes each side or until golden and cooked through. Remove from pan; cover to keep warm. Repeat with remaining oil and fritter mixture, to make 12 fritters in total.
5 Serve fritters topped with relish and rocket.

carrot relish Heat oil in a large frying pan over medium-high heat; cook garlic and chilli flakes for 30 seconds. Add carrot; cook for 3 minutes. Stir in currants, norbu, vinegar, the water and cardamom; cook for 6 minutes or until liquid has evaporated. Stir in tomatoes; cook a further 2 minutes or until softened slightly. Season. Cool.

nutritional count per serving 28.5g total fat (6g saturated fat); 1606kJ (384 cal); 17.7g carbohydrate; 10g protein; 8g fibre

tip The relish can be stored for up to 2 weeks in an airtight container in the fridge.

MAPLE & DIJON DRESSING

PREP TIME 5 MINUTES MAKES ⅔ CUP

Whisk ¼ cup macadamia oil, ¼ cup apple cider vinegar,
2 tablespoons pure maple syrup and 1 tablespoon dijon
mustard in a small bowl until combined. Season to taste.

tips Store in a sealed jar in the fridge for up to 1 month.
You could substitute olive oil for macadamia oil.
serving suggestion Serve with a salad of mixed leaves, or
beef and beetroot (beet), or chicken and haloumi, or lamb
and roast sweet potato.

HEALTHY CAESAR DRESSING

PREP TIME 5 MINUTES MAKES 1 CUP

Blend or process 1 cup yoghurt, 2 tablespoons olive oil,
2 tablespoons finely grated parmesan, 4 finely chopped
anchovies, ½ crushed garlic clove, 1 tablespoon lemon juice
and 3 teaspoons dijon mustard until smooth. Season to taste.

tip Store in a sealed jar in the fridge for up to 1 week.
serving suggestion Serve with a caesar salad of cos lettuce,
hard-boiled egg, parmesan and crisp bacon or avocado.

DRESSINGS

LEMON, AVOCADO & DILL DRESSING

PREP TIME 10 MINUTES MAKES 1½ CUPS

Blend or process 1 medium (250g) avocado, ¼ cup yoghurt, 2 tablespoons avocado oil, ⅓ cup water, ⅓ cup loosely packed fresh dill sprigs and ¼ cup of lemon juice until smooth. Season to taste. For a thinner consistency, add a little more water if necessary.

tip Store in a sealed jar in the fridge for up to 1 week.
serving suggestion Serve with a salad of iceberg lettuce and soft-boiled egg, or poached chicken and pistachio, or smoked salmon.

RASPBERRY & WHITE BALSAMIC VINAIGRETTE

PREP TIME 5 MINUTES MAKES ½ CUP

Push ½ cup fresh or thawed frozen raspberries through a fine sieve into a small bowl, using the back of a spoon. Whisk in ¼ cup white balsamic vinegar, 2 tablespoons macadamia oil and 1 teaspoon norbu (monk fruit sugar) or stevia granules. Season to taste.

tip Store in a sealed jar in the fridge for up to 1 week.
serving suggestion Serve with a salad of roast duck, slow cooked lamb or grilled chicken.

PERSIAN SABZI PUMPKIN SALAD

PREP + COOK TIME 1 HOUR SERVES 4

1.2kg (2½ pounds) jap pumpkin

⅓ cup (80ml) extra virgin olive oil

2 teaspoons finely grated lemon rind

2 tablespoons lemon juice

4 radishes (60g), sliced thinly

2 green onions (scallions), sliced thinly

¼ cup loosely packed fresh basil leaves

¼ cup loosely packed fresh coriander (cilantro) leaves

¼ cup loosely packed fresh mint leaves

¼ cup fresh dill sprigs

4 lebanese flatbread pockets (320g)

1 cup (280g) store-bought labne

250g (8 ounces) baby roma (egg) tomatoes, sliced crossways (see tips)

⅓ cup (45g) coarsely chopped pistachios

advieh spice mix

2 teaspoons dried rose petals

1 teaspoon caraway seeds

1 teaspoon ground cinnamon

1 teaspoon ground nutmeg

1 teaspoon ground cardamon

½ teaspoon ground cumin

½ teaspoon ground cloves

1 Preheat oven to 220°C/425°F. Line two oven trays with baking paper.

2 Make advieh spice mix.

3 Wash, halve and remove seeds from pumpkin; cut into 12 wedges. Divide wedges between oven trays. Drizzle with 2 tablespoons of the oil, season on both sides with 2 teaspoons advieh spice mix and salt and pepper. Bake for 40 minutes or until pumpkin is golden and skin is crisp at the edges.

4 Whisk remaining oil with rind and juice in a small bowl; season to taste.

5 Soak radish and green onion in ice-cold water for 5 minutes; drain, dry on paper towel. Place radish and green onion in a medium bowl with herbs; toss gently to combine.

6 Toast flatbreads in the oven for 3 minutes. Place breads on plates; spread with labne. Top with pumpkin, tomatoes and herb salad; sprinkle with pistachios, drizzle with dressing.

advieh spice mix Grind rose petals and caraway seeds with a mortar and pestle until a coarse powder. Stir in remaining spices.

nutritional count per serving 29.1g total fat (6.5g saturated fat); 2784kJ (666 cal); 77.4g carbohydrate; 18.3g protein; 10.6g fibre

tips Advieh is an aromatic Persian spice mix, that can be used to season vegetable, meat or fish dishes. You can make your own labne using the recipe on page 45. We used a mix of tomato varieties for extra colour; halve, quarter and slice the tomatoes depending on their size.

GREEN GAZPACHO
WITH PISTACHIO CROÛTONS

PREP + COOK TIME 30 MINUTES
(+ REFRIGERATION) SERVES 6

1 medium avocado (250g), chopped

50g (1½ ounces) baby spinach

360g (11½ ounces) honeydew melon, chopped coarsely

¼ cup loosely packed fresh basil leaves

2 cloves garlic, crushed

10 green onions (scallions), white part only, chopped coarsely

200g (6½ ounces) seedless green grapes

2 fresh long green chillies, chopped coarsely

750g (1½ pounds) green heirloom tomatoes, chopped coarsely

1 telegraph cucumber (400g), chopped coarsely

2 tablespoons white wine vinegar

¼ cup (60ml) extra virgin olive oil

8 ice cubes

¼ cup small fresh basil leaves, extra

pistachio croûtons

¼ cup (60ml) olive oil

1 clove garlic, crushed

4 slices seeded rye bread (260g), cut into 1cm (½-inch) cubes

¼ cup (35g) pistachios, chopped

1 Make pistachio croûtons.

2 Blend avocado, spinach, melon, basil, garlic, green onion, grapes, chilli, tomato and cucumber, in two batches. Strain through a fine sieve over a large bowl, pressing down to extract as much liquid as possible. Discard solids. Whisk in vinegar, half the oil and the ice cubes; season to taste. Refrigerate for 30 minutes or until chilled.

3 Serve gazpacho in chilled bowls or glasses, topped with croûtons, extra basil leaves and remaining oil.

pistachio croûtons Heat oil in a small frying pan over medium heat; cook garlic for 30 seconds. Add bread and pistachios; cook, stirring, for 5 minutes or until golden. Remove from pan; cool.

nutritional count per serving 29.3g total fat (5.2g saturated fat); 1739kJ (416 cal); 27.7g carbohydrate; 7.4g protein; 6.9g fibre

tip The gazpacho can be made up to 2 days ahead, store in an airtight container in the fridge; stir before serving.

PRAWN CHU CHEE CURRY
WITH ROTI BREAD

PREP + COOK TIME 1 HOUR SERVES 6

2 cups (400g) medium-grain brown rice

1 litre (4 cups) water

½ teaspoon salt

¼ cup (60g) ghee

2½ tablespoons thai red curry paste

1kg (2 pounds) uncooked prawns (shrimp), peeled, deveined, with tails intact

6 fresh kaffir lime leaves

270ml coconut milk

1 cup (250ml) fish stock

2 tablespoons coconut sugar

2 tablespoons fish sauce

1 tablespoon tamarind puree

½ cup (85g) chopped fresh pineapple

225g (7 ounces) canned bamboo shoots, drained, rinsed

1 fresh long red chilli, seeded, shredded finely

roti bread

1 teaspoon raw honey

¾ cup (180ml) warm water

¼ cup (60ml) milk

⅓ cup (80ml) rice bran oil

1 egg

3 cups (450g) white spelt flour

1 teaspoon salt

60g (2 ounces) ghee

1 Make roti bread.

2 Rinse rice in a sieve under cold water until water runs clear. Place rice in a medium saucepan with the water and salt; bring to the boil. Reduce heat to low; cook, covered, for 25 minutes or until water is absorbed. Remove from heat; stand, covered, 5 minutes. Fluff with a fork and keep warm.

3 Meanwhile, heat a wok over medium-high heat. Add ghee and paste; cook, stirring, for 2 minutes. Add prawns and 3 crushed lime leaves; cook, stirring, for 2 minutes. Add coconut milk and stock; simmer for 5 minutes. Add sugar, sauce and tamarind. Stir in bamboo shoots and pineapple; cook a further 2 minutes or until warmed though.

4 Finely shred remaining lime leaves; combine with chilli. Sprinkle lime leaf mixture on curry; serve with rice and warm roti bread.

roti bread Dissolve honey in a jug with the water, milk and 2 tablespoons of the oil; whisk in egg. Process flour and salt until combined. With the motor operating, gradually add milk mixture; process until it forms a sticky dough. Knead dough on a floured surface for 2 minutes or until smooth. Divide into six portions; roll into balls. Place balls in a medium bowl with remaining oil, turn to coat well. Pat a ball of dough out on a lightly oiled surface until 20cm (8-inch) round. Using oiled hands, carefully stretch dough out from the center in a circular motion, until dough is translucent and forms a 40cm (16-inch) round (don't worry if the dough rips, this will add texture). Fold each side into the centre to form a 15cm (6-inch) square; do not press. Place on a baking-paper-lined oven tray. Repeat with remaining dough. Heat 2 teaspoons ghee in a large frying pan over medium heat; cook roti, in batches, for 2 minutes each side or until golden, adding remaining ghee with each batch.

nutritional count per serving 44.4g total fat (22.7g saturated fat); 4201kJ (1005 cal); 115.9g carbohydrate; 34.3g protein; 3.5g fibre

HERB-CRUSTED SALMON
WITH PICKLED VEG

PREP + COOK TIME 35 MINUTES (+ REFRIGERATION) SERVES 8

You will need to make the pickled veg a day ahead.
You can also cook the salmon a day ahead, if you like.

2 tablespoons olive oil

1.3kg (2¾-pound) salmon fillet, skinned, pin-boned

¼ cup each finely chopped fresh dill, chervil, mint and chives

2 cups (50g) watercress sprigs

pickled veg

2 cups (500ml) white wine vinegar

3 cups (750ml) water

2 tablespoons sea salt

¼ cup (50g) norbu (monk fruit sugar)

1 tablespoon pink peppercorns

4 bay leaves

½ cup fresh dill sprigs

3 fresh long red chillies, halved

170g (5½ ounces) asparagus, trimmed, halved

400g (12½ ounces) baby rainbow carrots, trimmed, scrubbed, halved lengthways

8 small radishes (120g), halved

250g (8 ounces) baby cucumbers, halved lengthways

horseradish yoghurt

1½ cups (420g) greek-style yoghurt

⅓ cup (90g) horseradish cream

1½ tablespoons finely chopped fresh dill

1 Make pickled veg.

2 Preheat oven to 180°C/350°F. Line a large oven tray with baking paper; drizzle with half the oil, season with salt and pepper. Position salmon on tray to fit; rub with remaining oil, season.

3 Combine herbs in a small bowl; press onto salmon to thickly coat. Bake for 15 minutes for medium-rare or until cooked to your liking.

4 Meanwhile, make horseradish yoghurt.

5 Serve salmon with pickled veg, watercress and horseradish yoghurt.

pickled veg Place vinegar and the water in a deep glass or ceramic rectangular dish; stir in salt and norbu until dissolved. Add remaining ingredients, ensuring vegetables are completely covered (add extra water if necessary). Cover; refrigerate overnight.

horseradish yoghurt Whisk ingredients in a small bowl. Season. Refrigerate until required.

nutritional count per serving 22g total fat (7.3g saturated fat); 1861kJ (444 cal); 13g carbohydrate; 44g protein; 4g fibre

tips The pickled veg can be made up to 1 week ahead. Store in an airtight container in the fridge. You can use black peppercorns instead of pink, ocean trout instead of salmon and any combination of soft-leaf herbs you prefer including flat-leaf parsley and tarragon.

MISO & GINGER

PREP 5 MINUTES MAKES ¾ CUP

Whisk ⅓ cup sake, ¼ cup orange juice, ¼ cup white (shiro) miso, 3 teaspoons finely grated ginger and 1 tablespoon raw honey in a small bowl until combined.

With salmon Combine salmon and marinade; refrigerate, covered, at least 2 hours. Pan-fry on each side until brown; finish cooking in the oven. Serve with brown rice, roasted eggplant and black sesame seeds.

With prawns Combine prawns and marinade; refrigerate, covered, at least 2 hours. Chargrill until cooked. Serve with vermicelli noodle salad.

With whole chicken Combine chicken and marinade. Roast in oven. Serve with roasted vegetables.

tip To prevent the marinade from sticking, line your frying pan, roasting pan or chargrill pan with baking paper.

STICKY BOURBON

PREP TIME 5 MINUTES MAKES 1½ CUPS

Whisk ½ cup tamari, ¼ cup olive oil, ¼ cup apple cider vinegar, ⅓ cup bourbon, ¼ cup pure maple syrup, 2 cloves crushed garlic in a small bowl until combined.

With pork or beef ribs Combine ribs and marinade; refrigerate, covered, for 4 hours or overnight. Roast, basting with marinade during cooking.

With chicken thigh fillets Combine fillets and marinade; refrigerate, covered, for 4 hours or overnight. Chargrill until cooked. Serve with roasted vegetables and quinoa salad.

MARINADES

LEMON GRASS & COCONUT

PREP TIME 10 MINUTES MAKES 1½ CUPS

Process 1 tablespoon coarsely chopped ginger, 1 thinly sliced stalk (white part only) lemon grass, 1 teaspoon ground turmeric, 1 teaspoon sea salt flakes, 2 chopped cloves garlic and 2 shallots until finely chopped. Add 270ml can coconut milk, 1 tablespoon fish sauce, 3 teaspoons finely grated lime rind and 1 tablespoon lime juice; process until combined.

With chicken thighs, drumsticks or tenderloins Combine chicken and marinade; refrigerate, covered, 4 hours or overnight. Chargrill or bake until cooked. Serve with asian greens, basmati rice and coriander.

With prawns Combine prawns and marinade; refrigerate, covered, for 1-2 hours. Chargrill until cooked. Serve with a mango, mint and macadamia salad.

CHILLI TERIYAKI

PREP TIME 5 MINUTES MAKES 1¼ CUPS

Whisk ½ cup soy sauce, ⅓ cup raw honey, ¼ cup apple cider vinegar, 2 teaspoons finely grated ginger, 1 seeded, finely chopped small red chilli and ½ teaspoon sesame oil in a small bowl until well combined.

With chicken breast or thigh fillets Combine chicken and marinade; refrigerate, covered, 2 hours or overnight. Thread onto skewers; chargrill or barbecue. Sprinkle with toasted sesame seeds. Serve with rice and asian greens.

With salmon Combine salmon and marinade; refrigerate, covered, for up to 4 hours. Pan-fry, grill or bake. Serve with an asian herb salad.

With beef stir-fry strips Combine beef with marinade; refrigerate, covered, for 2 hours or overnight. Stir-fry with green onions, broccolini and hokkien noodles.

EASTERN MASH-UP RAMEN

PREP + COOK TIME 2 HOURS (+ REFRIGERATION) SERVES 4

You will need to start this recipe a day ahead.

1 litre (4 cups) chicken stock

10g (½ ounce) dashino-moto stock powder (see tips)

3 cups (750ml) water

3 cloves garlic, sliced thinly

¼ cup (60ml) soy sauce

2 tablespoons sake

1 teaspoon norbu (monk fruit sugar) or stevia granules

20g (¾-ounce) piece fresh ginger, sliced

1 long fresh red chilli, quartered lengthways

300g (9½ ounces) buckwheat soba noodles

2 green onions (scallions), cut into thin strips

3 sheets toasted nori (seaweed), quartered

1 teaspoon black sesame seeds

tea eggs

3 cups (750ml) water

1 cup (250ml) soy sauce

¼ cup (20g) black tea leaves

4 star anise

rind of 1 mandarin

4 eggs, from the fridge

kimchi

250g (8 ounces) baby cucumbers (qukes)

¼ cup (50g) norbu (monk fruit sugar)

2 tablespoons salt

¼ cup (60ml) boiling water

2 green onions (scallions), chopped coarsely

1 teaspoon finely grated ginger

1 clove garlic

1 fresh long green chilli, sliced thinly

2 tablespoons rice vinegar *(continued next column)*

1 teaspoon fish sauce

1 tablespoon soy sauce

1½ tablespoons sesame seeds, toasted

1 Make tea eggs.

2 Place chicken stock, dashino-moto, the water, garlic, sauce, sake, norbu, ginger and chilli in a saucepan; bring to the boil. Reduce heat; simmer for 30 minutes.

3 Meanwhile, make kimchi.

4 Cook noodles in a saucepan of boiling water for 6 minutes or until just tender; drain.

5 Peel and halve tea eggs. Divide noodles and soup among bowls; top with eggs, kimchi, green onion and nori, sprinkle with black sesame seeds.

tea eggs Bring the water, sauce, tea, star anise and rind to the boil in a medium saucepan. Reduce heat; simmer 1 hour. Cool. Cook eggs in a small saucepan of boiling water for 7 minutes. Run eggs under cold water to stop them continuing to cook. Crack shell all over, but do not peel. Place eggs in cooled tea mixture. Cover; refrigerate overnight.

kimchi Cut cucumbers in half lengthways; cut crossways into 5mm (¼-inch) slices. Stir norbu, salt and the water until dissolved. Place cucumber and salt mixture in a plastic zip-top bag, expel air; seal. Lie bag flat for 30 minutes. Meanwhile, process remaining ingredients until finely chopped; spoon into a small bowl. Drain cucumbers; rinse, pat dry with paper towel. Add to bowl; toss to combine.

nutritional count per serving 9.6g total fat (2.4g saturated fat); 1124kJ (269 cal); 23.6g carbohydrate; 16g protein; 6.2g fibre

tips Dashino-moto stock powder is Japanese stock powder, made from bonito (tuna) and konbu (seaweed), it is used to make dashi a stock that forms the base of many recipes. Eggs can steep in the reduction for up to 48 hours for a deep rich flavour. The unpeeled eggs can be stored in an airtight container in the fridge for up to 4 days.

CHILLI LIME SNAPPER
WITH CORN SALSA SALAD

PREP + COOK TIME 35 MINUTES SERVES 4

¼ cup (60ml) olive oil

1 clove garlic, sliced thinly

1 fresh long green chilli, seeded, chopped finely

1 teaspoon finely grated lime rind

4 x 180g (5½-ounce) boneless, skinless snapper fillets

2 corn cobs (250g), husks removed

6 red radishes (90g), sliced thinly

45g (1½ ounces) snowpea sprouts, trimmed

1 green onion (scallion), sliced thinly

¼ cup fresh coriander (cilantro) leaves

1 tablespoon lime juice

1 tablespoon white balsamic vinegar or white vinegar

1 tablespoon olive oil, extra

1 medium avocado (250g), sliced

lime wedges, to serve

1 Combine 2 tablespoons of the oil with garlic, chilli and rind in a small bowl; add snapper, turn to coat. Set aside.
2 Brush corn with remaining oil; cook on a heated chargrill plate (or barbecue), turning every 2 minutes, for 8 minutes or until corn is cooked and lightly charred. Cool.
3 Place radish, sprouts, green onion and coriander in a bowl of iced water to crisp.
4 Cut kernels from cooled cobs; place in a large bowl with juice, vinegar and extra oil. Remove radish mixture from water with a slotted spoon; drain on paper towel. Add to corn mixture, season to taste; toss gently to combine.
5 Line the chargrill plate with baking paper (ensure paper doesn't extend over the edge); cook snapper on heated plate, for 2 minutes each side or until just cooked through.
6 Serve snapper with corn salsa salad, avocado and lime.

nutritional count per serving 32.3g total fat (6g saturated fat); 2465kJ (589 cal); 25.5g carbohydrate; 44.5g protein; 8.9g fibre

tip You can use any fish fillets you like or even prawns for this recipe.

BROAD BEAN TARTINE

PREP + COOK TIME 35 MINUTES SERVES 4

200g (6½ ounces) cherry truss tomatoes

100g (3 ounces) mixed cherry tomatoes, halved

⅓ cup (80ml) olive oil

300g (9½ ounces) frozen broad (fava) beans

4 large thick slices seeded rye sourdough (260g)

1 buffalo mozzarella (250g), torn into pieces

¼ cup loosely packed fresh baby mint leaves

2 tablespoons fresh oregano leaves

1 teaspoon finely grated lemon rind (see tip)

1 clove garlic, crushed

1 tablespoon sherry vinegar

80g (2½ ounces) prosciutto

½ cup snow pea tendrils

1 Preheat oven to 200°C/400°F. Line an oven tray with baking paper.

2 Make a small cut in the base of each whole tomato; squeeze out seeds. Combine all tomatoes with 1 tablespoon of the oil in a small bowl; season. Place on tray; roast for 10 minutes or until tomatoes are blistered and softened.

3 Meanwhile, cook broad beans in a saucepan of boiling water for 1 minute; drain, cool under cold running water. Peel away the skins.

4 Brush bread slices with 2 tablespoons of the olive oil; season. Place bread on a hot chargrill plate (or under the grill), for 2 minutes each side or until lightly charred.

5 Place broad beans and roasted tomatoes in a medium bowl with mozzarella, herbs, rind, garlic, vinegar and remaining oil; season. Toss to combine.

6 Just before serving, place prosciutto, broad bean salad and snow pea tendrils on grilled bread.

nutritional count per serving 36.3g total fat (13g saturated fat); 2571kJ (615 cal); 33.4g carbohydrate; 33.8g protein; 4g fibre

tip If you have one, use a zester to cut the lemon rind into long thin strips.

SMOKY BARBECUE SAUCE

PREP + COOK TIME 35 MINUTES
MAKES 1½ CUPS

Heat 1 tablespoon olive oil in a medium saucepan over medium-high heat; cook 1 finely chopped medium (150g) brown onion for 5 minutes or until softened. Add 2 coarsely chopped cloves garlic and 1 tablespoon smoked paprika; cook until fragrant. Add 2 teaspoons finely grated ginger, 1 tablespoon tomato paste, 1 tablespoon dijon mustard, ¼ cup maple syrup, ¼ cup apple cider vinegar and 400g (12½ ounces) canned crushed tomatoes. Simmer, uncovered for 20 minutes or until thickened. Blend sauce until smooth; season to taste. Cool.

serving suggestion Serve with grilled lamb, chicken, beef or pork.

COCONUT SATAY SAUCE

PREP + COOK TIME 10 MINUTES
MAKES 1½ CUPS

Heat 1 tablespoon olive oil in a medium saucepan over medium heat; cook 1 teaspoon finely grated ginger, 1 finely chopped small fresh red chilli and 1 clove crushed garlic, for 2 minutes or until fragrant. Add ½ cup crunchy unsalted natural peanut butter, 3 teaspoons soy sauce, 1 teaspoon fish sauce and 1 teaspoon coconut sugar or stevia granules; stir over medium heat. Gradually whisk in 270ml canned coconut cream until combined; cook for 3 minutes or until combined. Stir in 1 tablespoon lime juice.

serving suggestion Serve with chicken or beef skewers or gado gado.

HONEY CHILLI SAUCE

PREP + COOK TIME 45 MINUTES
MAKES 1 CUP

Coarsely chop 4 fresh long red chillies. Remove seeds from 12 fresh long red chillies; coarsely chop. Process all chillies with 2 cloves garlic until finely chopped. Transfer to a medium saucepan; add 1¾ cups apple cider vinegar, ¾ cup raw honey and ¼ cup water; cook, stirring, for 5 minutes over low heat until honey melts. Increase heat, bring to a simmer; cook, stirring occasionally, for 20 minutes or until sauce thickens (sauce will thicken further on cooling). Cool.

tip Store in an airtight container, in the fridge, for up to 1 month.
serving suggestion Serve with grilled chicken, prawns, fish, calamari or prawns.

TOMATO KETCHUP

PREP + COOK TIME 1 HOUR 15 MINUTES
MAKES 2 CUPS

Heat 1 tablespoon olive oil in a medium saucepan; cook 1 coarsely chopped small (80g) brown onion 5 minutes or until softened. Add 800g (1½ pounds) canned diced tomatoes and ½ cup apple cider vinegar; bring to a boil. Reduce heat to a simmer; stir in 2 tablespoons tomato paste, 2 tablespoons maple syrup, 1 teaspoon sea salt flakes, ½ teaspoon ground cloves, 1 teaspoon ground allspice, ¼ teaspoon cayenne pepper. Simmer over low heat 1 hour or until sauce reduces and thickens. For a smooth sauce, blend with a stick blender. Cool.

serving suggestion Serve with beef, chicken or lamb burgers and sweet potato fries.

SAUCES

SWEET POTATO GNOCCHI
WITH ROASTED TOMATO SAUCE

PREP + COOK TIME 2 HOURS SERVES 4

580g (1¼ pounds) purple-skinned white-fleshed sweet potato

170g (5½ ounces) fresh firm ricotta

½ cup (40g) finely grated parmesan

1 teaspoon ground nutmeg

1 teaspoon sea salt

1 egg

1 cup (150g) white spelt flour

2 tablespoons olive oil

¼ cup (20g) flaked parmesan

¼ cup loosely packed small fresh basil leaves

roasted tomato sauce

500g (1 pound) vine-ripened tomatoes, halved

6 cloves garlic, unpeeled

1 large red capsicum (bell pepper) (350g), chopped coarsely

1 medium red onion (170g), cut into wedges

1 tablespoon fresh oregano leaves

1 tablespoon fresh lemon thyme leaves

1 tablespoon fresh rosemary leaves

¼ cup (60ml) extra virgin olive oil

2 tablespoons sugar-free balsamic vinegar

1 teaspoon pure maple syrup

¼ cup loosely packed fresh basil leaves

¼ cup (20g) finely grated parmesan

1 Preheat oven to 200°C/400°F.

2 Wrap sweet potato in foil; bake for 1½ hours or until tender.

3 Meanwhile, make roasted tomato sauce.

4 Combine ricotta, grated parmesan, nutmeg, salt and egg in a large bowl until smooth. Cut sweet potato in half lengthways; spoon flesh into a small bowl, mash with a fork. Add hot sweet potato to ricotta mixture; combine well. Stir flour into sweet potato mixture to form a firm dough.

5 Bring a large saucepan of salted water to the boil. Divide dough into eight portions. Using floured hands, roll each portion on a floured surface into a 2cm (¾-inch) thick sausage shape; cut into 4cm (1½-inch) lengths. Squeeze gnocchi in the middle to form a bow shape. Place gnocchi, in a single layer, on an oven tray dusted with flour.

6 Cook gnocchi in boiling water, in three batches, for 2 minutes or until they float to the surface. Remove with a slotted spoon to an oiled tray. Reserve ½ cup gnocchi cooking water; stir into roasted tomato sauce.

7 Heat a large frying pan with olive oil over high heat; cook gnocchi, tossing occasionally, for 5 minutes or until lightly golden. Stir sauce into gnocchi to combine. Serve gnocchi topped with flaked parmesan and basil.

roasted tomato sauce Line a large roasting pan with baking paper. Add tomatoes, garlic, capsicum, onion, herbs and 2 tablespoons of the oil; season, toss to coat. Roast for 1 hour or until vegetables are very tender. Squeeze garlic from skins onto vegetables. Transfer mixture to a medium saucepan, add vinegar, syrup, remaining oil, basil and parmesan; season. Using a stick blender, blend sauce until smooth. Keep warm over a low heat.

nutritional count per serving 34.2g total fat (10g saturated fat); 2725kJ (652 cal); 59.1g carbohydrate; 23.3g protein; 6g fibre

GLAZED CHICKEN
ON NOODLES

PREP + COOK TIME 1 HOUR SERVES 4

4 chicken breast supremes (720g) (see tips)

2 tablespoons rice bran oil

1 medium mandarin (200g), unpeeled, cut into four thick slices

4 cloves garlic, sliced thinly

2 long fresh red chillies, seeded, cut into matchsticks

300g (9½ ounces) leeks, trimmed, cut into matchsticks

270g (8½ ounces) dried udon noodles

2 green onions (scallions), sliced on the diagonal

¼ cup fresh coriander (cilantro) sprigs

glaze

⅓ cup (80ml) soy sauce

⅓ cup (80ml) chinese cooking wine (shao hsing)

2½ tablespoons raw honey

2 teaspoons finely grated mandarin rind

⅓ cup (80ml) mandarin juice

2 teaspoons finely grated ginger

½ teaspoon ground cinnamon

¼ teaspoon ground star anise

1 Preheat oven to 200°C/400°F. Line an oven tray with baking paper.

2 Make glaze.

3 Rub chicken with half the oil; season. Heat a large non-stick frying pan over medium heat; cook chicken for 5 minutes each side or until skin is golden. Transfer chicken to tray; brush glaze on both sides. Dip mandarin slices in glaze; place on chicken. Bake for 15 minutes, brushing with glaze halfway though cooking, or until chicken is cooked through. Cover; keep warm.

4 Heat remaining oil in same frying pan over medium heat; cook garlic and chilli for 1 minute. Add leek; cook for a further 5 minutes or until soft.

5 Meanwhile, cook noodles in a saucepan of boiling water for 10 minutes or until tender; drain, reserving ¼ cup cooking water.

6 Add noodles and reserved cooking water to pan with green onion and coriander; season, then toss to coat. Divide noodle mixture among shallow serving bowls; top with chicken and mandarin, drizzle with remaining glaze.

glaze Bring ingredients to a simmer in a small saucepan; cook for 5 minutes or mixture thickens.

nutritional count per serving 30.7g total fat (7.8g saturated fat); 2649kJ (633 cal); 40.4g carbohydrate; 47g protein; 4.7g fibre

tips Chicken breast supreme is a chicken breast with the skin and wing bone attached. Ask the butcher to prepare it for you or use skinless chicken breast fillets instead. You can use any Asian-style noodles you prefer. Toss the noodles with 1 teaspoon rice bran oil after cooking if you are not using them immediately.

QUINOA CRUSTED
KALE & FIG TART

**PREP + COOK TIME 1 HOUR 30 MINUTES
(+ REFRIGERATION) SERVES 6**

¾ cup (150g) tri-coloured quinoa, rinsed

1½ cups (120g) finely grated pecorino cheese

3 eggs

1 teaspoon sea salt flakes

1 tablespoon olive oil

1 clove garlic, crushed

3 cups (70g) firmly packed coarsely chopped kale

¼ cup (60ml) water

1 tablespoon dijon mustard

¾ cup (180ml) pouring cream

10 medium figs (600g), torn in half

1 cup (40g) loosely packed rocket (arugula) leaves

¼ cup (35g) roasted hazelnuts, halved

yoghurt dressing

⅓ cup (95g) greek-style yoghurt

1 teaspoon raw honey

2 teaspoons chopped fresh tarragon

½ clove garlic, crushed

1 Grease an 11cm x 35cm (4½-inch x 14-inch) rectangular loose-based tart tin.

2 Cook quinoa in a large saucepan of boiling water for 12 minutes or until tender; drain well. Cool.

3 Process quinoa and half the pecorino until quinoa is finely chopped. Add 1 egg and half the salt; process until mixture forms a coarse dough. Press mixture evenly over base and sides of tart tin. Refrigerate for 30 minutes or until firm.

4 Meanwhile, preheat oven to 200°C/400°F.

5 Bake tart shell for 30 minutes or until golden. Remove from oven; reduce temperature to 180°C/350°F.

6 Meanwhile, heat oil in a medium frying pan over medium heat; cook garlic for 30 seconds. Add kale; cook, stirring, for 30 seconds. Add the water; cook, covered, for 3 minutes. Remove from heat; stand, covered, for 1 minute. Cool; drain away any excess liquid.

7 Place kale mixture in a medium bowl with remaining eggs and salt, half the remaining pecorino, the mustard and cream; whisk to combine. Spread mixture evenly into tart shell; sprinkle with remaining pecorino.

8 Bake tart for 30 minutes or until filling is set. Place figs, cut-side up, on an oiled oven tray; bake alongside tart, for 30 minutes or until just soft.

9 Make yoghurt dressing.

10 Serve tart topped with figs, rocket and hazelnuts; drizzle with dressing.

yoghurt dressing Combine ingredients in a small bowl; season to taste.

nutritional count per serving 28g total fat (12.6g saturated fat); 1852kJ (442 cal); 30g carbohydrate; 16.5g protein; 4.5g fibre

ICED GREEN TEA & CUCUMBER SIPPER

PREP TIME 5 MINUTES (+ REFRIGERATION)
MAKES 1 LITRE (4 CUPS)

Brew 2 green tea bags in 3½ cups boiling water for 5 minutes. Stir in 1 tablespoon honey until dissolved. Cool in the fridge. Half fill a large jug with ice, then add ½ cup cucumber juice (see tip), 1 tablespoon lime juice, ½ cup crushed fresh mint leaves, 1 thinly sliced (130g) lebanese cucumber, ½ thinly sliced (75g) pink lady apple and the chilled green tea; stir to combine.

tip You will need to juice 2 medium (260g) lebanese cucumbers for the amount of juice required here. If you don't have a juicer, use a blender; strain mixture through a fine sieve.

ICED ALMOND CHAI TEA

PREP + COOK TIME 25 MINUTES
(+ REFRIGERATION) MAKES 1.25 LITRES (5 CUPS)

Place 3 cups water in a large saucepan with 2 teaspoons black tea leaves, 2 cinnamon sticks, 1 vanilla bean split lengthways, 1 tablespoon raw honey, 5 thick slices ginger, 6 cloves, 8 bruised cardamon pods, ½ teaspoon black peppercorns and 3 x 5cm (2-inch) strips orange rind; bring to the boil. Reduce heat; simmer for 20 minutes or until reduced to 1 cup. Remove from heat; refrigerate until chilled. Fill four tall glasses with ice cubes; pour ¼ cup of chai mix into each glass (or strain first if you prefer). Pour 1 cup almond milk into each glass.

tip Store the chai mix in the fridge for up to 2 weeks.

DRINKS

CHAMOMILE & LEMON SLEEPY TIME ICED TEA

PREP + COOK TIME 25 MINUTES (+ REFRIGERATION) MAKES 1 LITRE (4 CUPS)

Chamomile tea is known for its soothing and calming effect, making this the perfect bedtime drink.

Bring 1.25 litres (5 cups) of water to the boil in a medium saucepan; remove from heat. Add ⅓ cup dried chamomile flowers (or 3 tea bags), ¼ cup fresh lemon thyme sprigs and 4 slices lemon. Stir in 1 tablespoon raw honey until honey dissolves. Cover; steep for 20 minutes. Strain tea; refrigerate for at least 1 hour or until cooled. Serve tea mixture over ice with slices of lemon and extra sprigs fresh lemon thyme.

STRAWBERRY & BASIL SUNSHINE ICED TEA

PREP + COOK TIME 10 MINUTES (+ REFRIGERATION) MAKES 1.25 LITRES (5 CUPS)

White tea is one of the least processed of all teas; buds and leaves are allowed to dry naturally before being processed to produce a delicate taste.

Bring 1 litre (4 cups) water to the boil in a medium saucepan; remove from heat. Add 3 white tea bags and ½ cup fresh basil leaves; cover, steep for 5 minutes. Remove and discard basil and tea bags. Cool tea in the refrigerator. Blend 250g (8 ounces) ripe, hulled strawberries, ¼ cup of the cooled infused tea and 2 teaspoons stevia granules until smooth; strain through a fine sieve to remove seeds. Stir strawberry puree into remaining cooled tea with 2 tablespoons lemon juice. Half fill a large jug with ice, top with 2 sprigs fresh basil and 10 halved strawberries; stir in tea mixture.

HEALTHY KEDGEREE

PREP + COOK TIME 50 MINUTES SERVES 4

1.5 litres (6 cups) water

3 x 200g (6½-ounce) skinless, boneless salmon fillets

2 cups (400g) medium-grain brown rice

4 eggs, at room temperature

¼ cup (60ml) olive oil

1 medium brown onion (150g), chopped finely

2 cloves garlic, crushed

1 teaspoon finely grated fresh ginger

1½ tablespoons jalfrezi curry paste

2 tablespoons water, extra

1 cup (50g) loosely packed baby spinach

1 fresh long red chilli, sliced thinly

½ cup loosely packed fresh coriander (cilantro)

2 medium limes (180g), cut into wedges

½ cup (140g) greek-style yoghurt

1 Bring the water to the boil in a medium saucepan over high heat. Add salmon; reduce heat to low, simmer for 5 minutes or until salmon is just cooked. Remove salmon from water; keep warm. Reserve cooking water.

2 Add rice to reserved cooking water; bring to the boil. Reduce heat; simmer, uncovered, for 25 minutes or until tender. (If the rice becomes too dry during cooking, add ½ cup water.)

3 Meanwhile, place eggs in a small saucepan of cold water; bring to the boil. Boil for 7 minutes; drain, rinse under cold running water. Peel eggs; cut in half.

4 Heat 2 tablespoons of the oil in a large, deep frying pan over medium heat; cook onion, stirring occasionally, for 8 minutes or until onion has softened. Add garlic, ginger and curry paste; cook for 4 minutes or until paste has darkened slightly. Fold through rice with remaining oil, the extra water, spinach, flaked salmon and eggs; cook for 2 minutes or until spinach is wilted and salmon is heated through. Season to taste.

5 Serve kedgeree topped with chilli, coriander and lime; serve with yoghurt.

nutritional count per serving 44.7g total fat (10.8g saturated fat); 4163kJ (996 cal); 84.9g carbohydrate; 60g protein; 5.6g fibre

tip Jalfrezi curry paste is available from Asian food stores.

PRAWN & CRAB
SWEET POTATO SLIDERS

PREP + COOK TIME 35 MINUTES MAKES 12

The sweet potatoes need to be about 7cm (2¾ inches) in diameter, as they will serve as the 'buns' for the sliders.

3 purple-skinned white-fleshed sweet potatoes (1kg), unpeeled

¼ cup (60ml) olive oil

12 large green king prawns (shrimp) (300g), peeled, deveined, with tails intact

2 cups (50g) watercress sprigs

¼ cup fresh micro sorrel leaves

¼ cup fresh coriander (cilantro) leaves

1 tablespoon extra virgin olive oil

1 tablespoon lemon juice

1 medium avocado (250g)

crab filling

200g (6½ ounces) cooked crab meat

½ cup (60g) crème fraîche

½ clove garlic, crushed

1 green onion (scallions), chopped finely

1 tablespoon finely chopped fresh chives

1 tablespoon nigella seeds

2 tablespoons horseradish cream

1 tablespoon lemon juice

1 Cut eight 8mm (½-inch) thick rounds, from each sweet potato (you need 24 rounds in total); discard tapered ends. Brush rounds with 2 tablespoons of the olive oil; season. Cook rounds, in batches, on a heated chargrill plate (or barbecue) for 6 minutes each side or until cooked through. Remove from heat; keep warm.

2 Make crab filling.

3 Coat prawns in remaining olive oil; season. Cook prawns on heated chargrill plate for 1 minute each side or until just cooked through. remove from heat; cover to keep warm.

4 Place watercress, sorrel and coriander in a small bowl with extra virgin olive oil and juice. Season; toss to combine. Mash avocado in a small bowl.

5 Place 12 sweet potato rounds on a board; top each with crab filling, a prawn, mashed avocado and watercress salad. Top with remaining sweet potato rounds.

crab filling Combine ingredients in a small bowl; season.

nutritional count per slider 13g total fat (3.2g saturated fat); 903kJ (216 cal); 15.1g carbohydrate; 8.4g protein; 3g fibre

tip We used crème fraîche in the crab filling rather than a commercial aïoli or mayonnaise, as they tend to contain refined sugars.

OLIVE CHICKEN WITH
MAPLE ROASTED VEGETABLES

PREP + COOK TIME 1 HOUR 50 MINUTES SERVES 4

¼ cup (60ml) olive oil

1 whole chicken (1.6kg), cut into 10 pieces

1 medium brown onion (150g), chopped coarsely

2 cloves garlic, crushed

3 sprigs fresh thyme

18 sicilian green olives (90g)

1 litre (4 cups) chicken stock

1 tablespoon lemon juice

maple roasted vegetables

600g (1¼ pounds) kent pumpkin, cut into
2cm (¾-inch) wedges

4 small parsnips (480g), unpeeled, quartered
lengthways

400g (12½ ounces) spring onions, trimmed to
10cm (4-inch) lengths, quartered lengthways

2 tablespoons extra virgin olive oil

2 tablespoons pure maple syrup

1 cup (40g) loosely packed rocket (arugula) leaves

1 tablespoon lemon juice

1 Heat oil in a large heavy-based saucepan over high heat; cook chicken, in batches, for 2 minutes each side or until browned. Remove from pan.

2 Reduce heat of same pan to medium; cook onion, garlic, thyme and olives, stirring occasionally, for 5 minutes or until onion is softened. Increase heat to high; return chicken and any juices to pan. Add stock; bring to the boil. Reduce heat to low; simmer, covered, for 1 hour or until chicken is cooked through. Remove chicken from pan.

3 Meanwhile, preheat oven to 200°C/400°F; make maple roasted vegetables.

4 Increase saucepan heat to high; bring to the boil. Reduce heat slightly; cook, uncovered, for 20 minutes or until liquid has reduced to 1 cup (250ml). Add juice, season to taste.

5 Serve chicken with reduced mixture and vegetables.

maple roasted vegetables Line two oven trays with baking paper. Divide pumpkin, parsnip and onion between trays; drizzle with oil and maple syrup, season, then toss to coat. Roast for 40 minutes, turning halfway through cooking or until vegetables are tender. Combine rocket and lemon juice in a medium bowl; season to taste. Just before serving, toss rocket through vegetables.

nutritional count per serving 57.1g total fat (13.1g saturated fat); 3758kJ (899 cal); 36.3g carbohydrate; 57g protein; 10g fibre

tip These olives contain pits, so warn your guests before eating. Alternatively use pitted olives.

3PM SLUMP

076   077

BLISS BALLS

PREP TIME 20 MINUTES MAKES 42 (14 EACH)

apricot & tahini

½ cup (100g) dried apricots

¼ cup (30g) linseed (flaxseed) meal

1 cup (160g) almond kernels

¼ green apple (30g), unpeeled, grated coarsely

1 tablespoon raw honey, rice malt syrup or pure maple syrup

1 tablespoon hulled tahini (sesame seed paste)

¼ teaspoon orange blossom water, optional

½ cup (40g) shredded coconut

fig & hazelnut

1 cup (140g) roasted skinned hazelnuts

100g (3 ounces) dried figs

¼ cup (30g) linseed (flaxseed) meal

¼ green apple (30g), grated coarsely

¼ teaspoon ground cinnamon

2 tablespoons white chia seeds

date & cacao nibs

100g (3 ounces) fresh dates, pitted

1 cup (160g) almond kernels

¼ cup (35g) cacao nibs

¼ green apple (30g), grated coarsely

2 teaspoons dutch-processed cocoa

2 teaspoons dutch-processed cocoa, extra

1 For apricot and tahini balls, process apricots, linseed, almonds and apple for 1 minute or until mixture is the consistency of breadcrumbs. Add honey, tahini and orange blossom water; process a further minute or until mixture clings together when pressed.

2 Roll tablespoons of the mixture into balls; wet your hands every third or fourth ball to stop the mixture from sticking. Coat balls in coconut.

3 Make fig and hazelnut balls, then date and cacao balls.

fig & hazelnut Process hazelnuts with figs, linseed meal, apple and cinnamon for 2 minutes or until mixture starts to clump together. Roll tablespoons of the mixture into balls then coat in chia seeds.

date & cacao nibs Process dates with almonds, cacao nibs, apple and cocoa for 2 minutes or until mixture starts to clump together. Roll tablespoons of the mixture into balls then dust with extra cocoa.

nutritional count per apricot & tahini ball 9.9g total fat (2.2g saturated fat); 573kJ (136 cal); 8.1g carbohydrate; 4.1g protein; 0.5g fibre

nutritional count per fig & hazelnut ball 7.8g total fat (0.4g saturated fat); 431kJ (103 cal); 4.8g carbohydrate; 2.5g protein; 2.6g fibre

nutritional count per date & cacao nibs ball 6.9g total fat (0.5g saturated fat); 451kJ (108 cal); 6.7g carbohydrate; 3.2g protein; 0.9g fibre

ROASTED RHUBARB &
BALSAMIC POPSICLES

PREP + COOK TIME 25 MINUTES (+ STANDING & FREEZING) MAKES 6

You need a six-hole ½-cup ice-block mould and six ice-block sticks for this recipe.

6 trimmed stalks rhubarb (330g), cut into 8cm (3¼-inch) lengths

1 vanilla bean, split lengthways, seeds scraped

1 tablespoon balsamic glaze

1 tablespoon raw honey or pure maple syrup

400ml coconut milk

¼ cup (90g) raw honey or pure maple syrup, extra

½ cup (80g) natural sliced almonds, chopped coarsely

chocolate coating

½ cup (100g) virgin coconut oil

2 tablespoons cocoa powder

1 teaspoon vanilla extract

2 teaspoons raw honey or pure maple syrup

1 Preheat oven to 200°C/400°F. Line an oven tray with baking paper.

2 Place rhubarb, vanilla seeds and pod on oven tray; drizzle with balsamic glaze and honey. Roast for 15 minutes or until tender; stand until cool. Discard vanilla pod.

3 Process or blend rhubarb mixture with coconut milk and extra honey until smooth. Pour into ice-block mould. Cover mould with a double layer of plastic wrap (this will help keep the ice-block sticks upright). Pierce plastic with a small knife, then push an ice-block stick into each hole. Freeze for 4 hours or until frozen.

4 When you're ready to coat the frozen popsicles, make chocolate coating.

5 Line an oven tray with baking paper; place in the freezer. Pour chocolate coating into a small, deep bowl. Place almonds in another small bowl. Dip popsicle moulds very briefly in boiling water; remove popsicles. Dip the popsicles halfway into the chocolate coating, then dip into nuts. Place on chilled tray. Freeze for 5 minutes or until coating is set.

chocolate coating Stir ingredients in a small saucepan over low heat until oil is melted and mixture is combined. Remove from heat; stand at room temperature until cool.

nutritional count per popsicle 38.3g total fat (28.2g saturated fat); 1910kJ (456 cal); 23.9g carbohydrate; 5.4g protein; 3.1g fibre

tips If the chocolate coating mixture thickens too much while dipping the popsicles, place it in a microwave-safe bowl and microwave on MEDIUM (50%) for 10 seconds. Don't worry if the chocolate coating has a slight whitish look to it, this is simply the coconut fat and won't affect the taste.

SALTED DATE
CARAMELS

**PREP + COOK TIME 20 MINUTES
(+ STANDING & FREEZING) MAKES 16**

2 cups (310g) fresh dates, pitted

¾ cup (150g) virgin coconut oil

¼ cup (25g) cacao powder

1 teaspoon vanilla extract

2 tablespoons virgin coconut oil, extra,
at room temperature

½ teaspoon sea salt flakes

¼ cup (50g) coconut flour

sea salt flakes, extra, for sprinkling

1 Place dates in a medium bowl, cover with boiling water;
stand for 10 minutes to soften. Drain dates; discard water.

2 Meanwhile, melt coconut oil in a small saucepan;
combine oil and sifted cacao in a small bowl. Stand until
thickened slightly.

3 Process dates with extract, extra coconut oil and salt
until smooth. Transfer mixture to a small bowl, cover;
freeze for 30 minutes or until firm.

4 Line an oven tray with baking paper. Place coconut flour
in a small bowl. Using damp hands, roll tablespoonfuls
of date mixture into balls. Roll balls in coconut flour.
Using a spoon, dip balls into cacao coating; place on tray.
Sprinkle with extra salt. Freeze for 10 minutes or until set.

nutritional count per ball 12.1g total fat (11.2g saturated
fat); 657kJ (157 cal); 12.6g carbohydrate; 1.3g protein;
1.2g fibre

tips Don't worry if the coating on the caramels has a slight
whitish look to it, this is simply the coconut fat and won't
affect the taste. Store and eat the caramels straight from the
freezer. Place the caramels in small paper cases to serve.

CHAI-SPICED
POPCORN

PREP + COOK TIME 10 MINUTES SERVES 4

¼ cup (60ml) olive oil

1 tablespoon powdered stevia or norbu (monk fruit sugar)

2 teaspoons ground cinnamon

1 teaspoon ground ginger

½ teaspoon ground cardamom

½ teaspoon ground allspice

½ teaspoon sea salt flakes

2 tablespoons olive oil, extra

½ cup (120g) popping corn

1 Combine oil, stevia, spices and salt in a small bowl.

2 Heat the extra oil in a large saucepan over medium heat. Add the popping corn, cover pan; cook, shaking the pan occasionally, for 5 minutes, or until popping stops.

3 Place popcorn in a large bowl; drizzle with spice mixture, stir until well coated.

nutritional count per serving 24.2g total fat (3.6g saturated fat); 1328kJ (317 cal); 25.6g carbohydrate; 3g protein; 0.7g fibre

tips If you have one, it's handy to use a saucepan with a glass lid so you can see if all the corn has popped. Popcorn can be made a day ahead; cool and store in an airtight container.

HOMEMADE CHOCOLATE
HAZELNUT SPREAD

PREP TIME 10 MINUTES **MAKES** 2 CUPS

1½ cups (210g) roasted hazelnuts, skins removed

¼ cup (25g) cacao powder

¼ teaspoon sea salt flakes

½ cup (125ml) unsweetened almond milk

⅓ cup (80ml) pure maple syrup

1 tablespoon vanilla extract

1 tablespoon virgin coconut oil

1 Blend ingredients for 5 minutes, scraping down the sides occasionally, until smooth.

2 Spoon spread into a small airtight container. Store in the fridge for up to 1 month.

nutritional count per tablespoon 30.7g total fat (5.7g saturated fat); 1545kJ (369 cal); 21.4g carbohydrate; 7.8g protein; 4.1g fibre

tips To roast the hazelnuts at home, spread nuts on an oven tray and roast at 180°C/350°F for 8 minutes or until golden. Rub warm hazelnuts in a clean tea towel to remove skins; cool. Use this spread as a filling for cakes or cookies, or spread onto bread.

RAW TURKISH
DELIGHT BARK

PREP TIME 10 MINUTES (+ REFRIGERATION) **SERVES** 10

1 cup (200g) virgin coconut oil

½ cup (50g) cacao powder

pinch sea salt

⅓ cup (115g) rice malt syrup

⅓ cup (50g) coarsely chopped raw almonds

⅓ cup (50g) dried cherries

¼ cup (4g) dried edible rose petals

1 Grease a 20cm x 30cm (8-inch x 12-inch) slice pan; line base with baking paper.

2 Whisk oil, sifted cacao and salt in a medium bowl until combined. Gradually add syrup, whisking to combine.

3 Spread mixture evenly into pan; sprinkle with nuts, cherries and rose petals. Refrigerate until set. Break into shards to serve.

nutritional count per serving 23.3g total fat (19.1g saturated fat); 1126kJ (269 cal); 14g carbohydrate; 2.4g protein; 0.4g fibre

tips Don't worry if the bark has a slight whitish look to it, this is simply the coconut fat and won't affect the taste. Because of the low melting point of the coconut oil, the bark should always be stored in the fridge otherwise it will be too soft to handle.

SPICED APPLE PIE
OAT SMOOTHIE

PREP TIME 5 MINUTES SERVES 2 (MAKES 1 LITRE)

As well as being a great afternoon pick-me-up, you can pour the smoothie into a large glass bottle and take to work for a breakfast on the go.

1 cup (90g) rolled oats

2 tablespoon maca powder (see tips)

1 cup (250ml) almond milk

1 cup (250ml) pure apple juice

2 small red apples (260g), cored, chopped coarsely

¼ cup (70g) greek-style yoghurt

4 fresh medjool dates (20g), pitted, chopped coarsely

1 teaspoon ground cinnamon

¼ teaspoon ground nutmeg

1 vanilla bean, split lengthways, seeds scraped

6 ice cubes

1 Place ingredients in a blender; blend until smooth.
2 Pour smoothie into tall glasses; sprinkle with a little extra ground cinnamon.

nutritional count per serving 19.9g total fat (3g saturated fat); 2174kJ (520 cal); 68.2g carbohydrate; 13.1g protein; 9g fibre

tips Maca powder is available from major supermarkets and health food stores. Maca is the root of a plant native to South America, where it has been consumed for several thousand years. It is a rich source of vitamin C, iron, copper and calcium, and a very good source of riboflavin, niacin, vitamin B6, potassium and manganese. It also contains about 14% protein and provides a good dose of fibre. Medjool dates are available from the fresh food section of major supermarkets. When pears are in season, use a juicy variety such as packham instead of the red apples and pear juice instead of apple juice.

GINGER & SESAME
SEED LOGS

PREP + COOK TIME 15 MINUTES (+ REFRIGERATION) **MAKES** 26

1 cup (100g) walnuts

1 cup (140g) macadamias

1 cup (90g) rolled oats

400g (12½ ounces) fresh medjool dates, pitted

1½ teaspoons ground ginger

½ teaspoon sea salt

½ cup (75g) sesame seeds

1 Process nuts and oats in a food processor until finely chopped. Add dates, ginger and salt; process until mixture forms a paste.

2 Shape level tablespoons of mixture into 5cm (2-inch) long logs; place on a baking-paper-lined oven tray. Refrigerate for 15 minutes.

3 Meanwhile, stir sesame seeds in a frying pan over medium heat for 2 minutes or until lightly toasted. Cool.

4 Roll logs in sesame seeds; place on a tray. Refrigerate for 2 hours or until firm.

nutritional count per log 8.6g total fat (0.9g saturated fat); 601kJ (143 cal); 14.5g carbohydrate; 2.3g protein; 1.2g fibre

tips Medjool dates are available from the fresh food section of major supermarkets. Store logs in an airtight container in the fridge for up to 2 weeks or freeze for up to 3 months.

BROWN RICE
ENERGY BALLS

PREP + COOK TIME 1 HOUR (+ REFRIGERATION) MAKES 12

Turn the energy balls into lunch, by stuffing them into a pitta pocket or wrap with salad ingredients and a little dressing made from greek-style yoghurt, a couple of teaspoons of tahini and lemon juice.

1 cup (200g) medium-grain brown rice

2½ cups (625ml) chicken stock

2 tablespoons tahini

1 tablespoon tamari

1 tablespoon apple cider vinegar

2 tablespoons chia seeds

2 green onions (scallions), chopped finely

2 teaspoons finely grated fresh ginger

2 tablespoons black sesame seeds

2 tablespoons white sesame seeds

1 Rinse rice under running water until water runs clear. Place rice in a medium saucepan with stock; bring to the boil. Reduce heat to low; cook, covered, for 40 minutes or until stock is almost absorbed and rice is tender. Remove from heat; stand, covered, for 5 minutes.

2 Transfer hot rice to a medium bowl; immediately stir in tahini, tamari, vinegar, chia seeds, green onion and ginger, season to taste. Stand for 5 minutes or until cool enough to handle.

3 Roll 2 tablespoons of mixture into balls; roll in combined sesame seeds. Place balls on a baking-paper-lined tray. Refrigerate at least 30 minutes before eating.

nutritional count per ball 6g total fat (0.7g saturated fat); 527kJ (126 cal); 13.4g carbohydrate; 3.7g protein; 2.1g fibre

tips As with meat, ingredients containing rice should always be kept refrigerated and never left at room temperature, otherwise food poisoning can occur. Rice balls will keep refrigerated for up to 5 days.

CHILLI
MISO SOUP

PREP + COOK TIME 15 MINUTES SERVES 2

¼ cup (75g) dashi miso paste

3 cups (750ml) water

150g (4½ ounces) silken tofu, cut into 1cm (½-inch) cubes

3 green onions (scallions), sliced thinly on the diagonal

1 fresh long red chilli, sliced thinly on the diagonal

2 toasted nori (seaweed) sheets, each cut into eight pieces

2 teaspoons black sesame seeds

1 Whisk dashi miso paste and water in a small saucepan. Bring to a simmer over medium heat.
2 Meanwhile, divide tofu, green onion, chilli and nori between two bowls.
3 Pour miso soup into bowls; sprinkle with sesame seeds. Serve immediately.

nutritional count per serving 5.4g total fat (0.9g saturated fat); 635kJ (152 cal); 12.4g carbohydrate; 12g protein; 2.2g fibre

TOASTED
NORI CHIPS

PREP + COOK TIME 15 MINUTES MAKES 60

2 teaspoons sesame seeds

1 teaspoon sea salt, crumbled

10 nori (seaweed) sheets

2 tablespoons sesame oil

nanami togarashi

1 tablespoon finely grated orange rind

2 teaspoons cracked black pepper

1 tablespoon chilli flakes

2 teaspoons black sesame seeds

1 Make nanami togarashi.

2 Crush sesame seeds using a mortar and pestle; combine with 2 teaspoons of the nanami togarashi and the salt. (Store remaining nanami togarashi for another use.)

3 Using scissors, cut each nori sheet into triangles or squares. Place on a large baking-paper-lined oven tray; lightly brush nori with sesame oil.

4 Heat a large non-stick frying pan over medium-high heat; toast nori, in batches, for 2 minutes each side or until crisp. Return to paper-lined tray; sprinkle immediately with nanami togarashi mixture.

nanami togarashi Dry-fry rind in a small frying pan over medium heat for 5 minutes or until rind is dry and crispy. Place in a screw-top jar with remaining ingredients; shake well to combine.

nutritional count per chip 0.6g total fat (0.1g saturated fat); 31kJ (7 cal); 0.1g carbohydrate; 0.2g protein; 0.02g fibre

tips Nanami togarashi is a Japanese seven-spice mix, also called shichimi togarashi (both nana and shichi mean seven in Japanese). The blend contains red peppers, sansho pepper, orange rind, black and white sesame seeds, seaweed and ginger. It is available from Asian food stores if you don't want to make your own.

ROASTED SWEET & SOUR
CHICKPEAS & BEANS

PREP + COOK TIME 1 HOUR   SERVES 4 (MAKES 2½ CUPS)

2 x 400g (12½ ounces) canned chickpeas (garbanzo beans)

2 x 400g (12½ ounces) canned butter beans

1 tablespoon extra virgin olive oil

1 tablespoon finely grated lime rind

2 teaspoons ground cumin

2 teaspoons ground coriander

1 teaspoon chilli flakes

1 tablespoon coconut sugar

1 Preheat oven to 220°C/425°F. Line an oven tray with baking paper.

2 Drain then rinse chickpeas and beans; place in a medium heatproof bowl. Cover with boiling water; drain. Dry on paper towel. (This will ensure that the chickpeas and beans will dry and crisp during roasting.)

3 Place chickpeas and beans on tray. Bake for 50 minutes, stirring occasionally, or until golden and crisp.

4 Transfer roasted chickpeas and beans to a medium bowl. Add oil, rind, cumin, coriander, chilli flakes and coconut sugar. Season generously with salt and freshly ground black pepper; toss until well coated.

nutritional count per serving 9.6g total fat (1.3g saturated fat); 1381kJ (330 cal); 37.4g carbohydrate; 17.9g protein; 15g fibre

tips You can use dried legumes instead: soak them overnight first and cook for 1½ hours in boiling water. Experiment with different spices and herbs to flavour how you like it. Store the roasted mix in an airtight container or jar for up to 4 days.

CHIA & TOMATO GUACAMOLE
WITH SUMAC CRISPS

PREP + COOK TIME 20 MINUTES SERVES 4

cooking oil spray

4 rye mountain breads (100g)

1½ teaspoons ground sumac

2 medium avocados (500g), chopped coarsely

⅓ cup (80ml) lime juice

1 small red onion (100g), chopped finely

⅓ cup (60g) semi-dried tomatoes, chopped finely

¼ cup fresh coriander (cilantro), chopped coarsely

½ teaspoon smoked paprika

1½ tablespoons black or white chia seeds

2 fresh long red chillies, sliced thinly

1 Preheat oven to 200°C/400°F. Line three oven trays with baking paper; spray with cooking oil.

2 Cut each sheet of mountain bread into 16 triangles. Place in a single layer on trays; spray with oil. Sprinkle with sumac; season with salt and pepper. Bake for 5 minutes or until golden and crisp.

3 Place avocado and juice in a medium bowl; mash lightly with a fork. Stir in red onion, tomato, coriander, paprika, 1 tablespoon chia seeds and three-quarters of the chilli. Season to taste with salt.

4 Place guacamole in a serving bowl; top with remaining chilli and remaining chia seeds. Serve with sumac crisps.

nutritional count per serving 23g total fat (4.7g saturated fat); 1391kJ (332 cal); 19g carbohydrate; 7.2g protein; 6.5g fibre

tips Guacamole can be stored, covered, in the fridge for up to 2 days. Sumac crisps will keep in an airtight container at room temperature for up to 1 week.

PAPAYA & MACADAMIA SALAD
WITH COCONUT YOGHURT

PREP + COOK TIME 15 MINUTES SERVES 2

1 small papaya (650g)

1 cup (280g) coconut yoghurt

¼ cup (35g) roasted macadamia halves

⅓ cup (15g) coconut flakes, toasted

2 teaspoons finely grated lime rind (see tip)

2 limes (180g), cut into wedges

1 Cut papaya in half lengthways; scoop out the seeds.
2 Spoon yoghurt into papaya hollow; sprinkle with macadamias, coconut and rind.
3 Serve immediately with lime wedges.

nutritional count per serving 41g total fat (24g saturated fat); 2052kJ (490 cal); 23.5g carbohydrate; 4.9g protein; 6.3g fibre

tip If you have one, use a zester to cut the lime rind into long thin strips.

CAULIFLOWER
PIZZA BITES

PREP + COOK TIME 45 MINUTES   MAKES 24

300g (9½ ounces) cauliflower florets, chopped

½ cup (60g) ground almonds

¼ cup (30g) finely grated vintage cheddar

1 teaspoon finely chopped fresh rosemary

1 teaspoon finely chopped fresh oregano

1 egg, beaten lightly

2 lebanese eggplants (160g)

2 medium zucchini (240g)

1 tablespoon olive oil

1 cup (150g) canned crushed tomatoes

1 clove garlic, crushed

20g (¾ ounce) fetta, crumbled

¼ cup (40g) pine nuts, toasted

2 tablespoons fresh oregano leaves, extra

1 Preheat oven to 220°C/425°F. Grease two flat-based 12-hole (2-tablespoon/40ml) patty pan trays; line bases with small rounds of baking paper.

2 Pulse cauliflower in a food processor until it resembles fine crumbs; transfer to a large bowl. Add ground almonds, cheddar, herbs and egg; season and combine well. Spoon mixture into holes; press firmly on base and side to form a tart shell. Bake 10 minutes or until golden and crisp. Leave oven on.

3 Meanwhile, use a mandoline or V-slicer to cut eggplant and zucchini into 3mm (⅛-inch) thick slices. Cook vegetables on a heated oiled chargrill plate (or grill), on one side only, for 2 minutes or until lightly charred. Transfer to a medium bowl, add oil and season; toss to coat.

4 Combine tomatoes and garlic in a small bowl. Spoon 1 teaspoon tomato mixture into each pizza bite; top with grilled vegetables and fetta.

5 Bake bites for 5 minutes or until fetta is golden. Loosen each pizza bite from the pan using a butter knife. Serve topped with extra pine nuts and oregano.

nutritional count per bite 4.2g total fat (0.7g saturated fat); 214kJ (51 cal); 0.9g carbohydrate; 1.9g protein; 1g fibre

tips You can use any leftover cheese you have in the fridge instead of cheddar. Make a double batch of bases; freeze half so you have them at the ready. Pizza bites can be made a day ahead and reheated in the microwave, on a plate lined with paper towel, on HIGH (100%) for 1 minute; stand 2 minutes before serving.

ZUCCHINI & BLUEBERRY LOAF CAKES

PREP + COOK TIME 45 MINUTES MAKES 8

3 medium zucchini (360g), grated coarsely

2¾ cups (300g) ground almonds

¾ cup (120g) coconut sugar

1 teaspoon ground cinnamon

½ teaspoon sea salt

2 teaspoons baking powder

½ cup (175g) pure maple syrup

½ cup (125ml) melted virgin coconut oil

3 eggs, beaten lightly

1 vanilla bean, split lengthways, seeds scraped

2 teaspoons finely grated orange rind

⅓ cup (80ml) orange juice

1 cup (150g) frozen blueberries

½ cup (25g) coconut flakes, toasted

1 Preheat oven 180°C/350°F. Grease an 8-hole (½ cup/125ml) loaf pan tray; line base and long sides of holes with strips of baking paper, extending the paper 3cm (1¼-inches) over long sides.

2 Squeeze liquid from zucchini; place zucchini in a large bowl. Add ground almonds, coconut sugar, cinnamon, salt and baking powder; stir to combine.

3 Whisk maple syrup, coconut oil, egg, vanilla seeds (reserve pod for another use), rind and juice in a small bowl. Add syrup mixture to zucchini mixture; stir gently to combine. Fold in blueberries. Spoon mixture into pan holes.

4 Bake loaves for 30 minutes or until risen and slightly cracked on top. Leave loaves in pan for 5 minutes before turning, top-side up, onto a wire rack to cool.

5 Brush loaves with a little extra maple syrup; sprinkle with toasted coconut.

nutritional count per loaf 39.2g total fat (16.3g saturated fat); 2227kJ (532 cal); 34.5g carbohydrate; 10.7g protein; 4.4g fibre

tips You can use any nut meal in this gluten-free recipe. Swap the blueberries for raspberries for a more tart taste. These cakes will keep in an airtight container for up to 3 days or in the freezer for up to 1 month.

MISO ALMOND BUTTER
WITH AVOCADO

PREP + COOK TIME 15 MINUTES SERVES 4

1½ tablespoons white (shiro) miso paste

2 tablespoons almond butter

2 tablespoons olive oil

½ teaspoon sesame oil

1 tablespoon mirin

1 tablespoon water

2 medium avocados (500g)

⅓ cup (50g) roasted cashews, chopped coarsely

½ teaspoon black sesame seeds

1 Stir miso, almond butter, oils, mirin and the water in a medium jug until smooth; season to taste.
2 Cut unpeeled avocados in half; discard stones. Spoon dressing into avocado hollow; sprinkle with cashews and sesame seeds. Serve immediately.

nutritional count per serving 42.7g total fat (7.5g saturated fat); 1829kJ (437 cal); 6.1g carbohydrate; 7.3g protein; 1.6g fibre

tips Use any of your favourite healthy dressings or dips for this quick and easy snack. The miso almond butter will keep in an airtight container and can also be used as a dressing for salads.

FROZEN
GREEN POWER BITES

PREP + COOK TIME 10 MINUTES (+ FREEZING) MAKES 25

3 ripe medium bananas (600g)

¼ cup (30g) ground almonds

½ cup (70g) chopped pitted dates

½ cup (80g) currants

¾ cup (90g) coarsely chopped pecans

¼ cup (35g) sesame seeds

¼ cup (25g) cacao powder

2 tablespoons coconut butter, melted

½ cup (40g) quinoa flakes

1 tablespoon spirulina powder

2 tablespoons barley malt syrup

25 mini wooden popsicle sticks

¼ cup (20g) shredded coconut

¼ cup (30g) coarsely chopped pecans, extra

1 Mash banana in a large bowl with a fork. Add ground almonds, dates, currants, pecans, sesame seeds, cacao, coconut butter, quinoa flakes, spirulina powder and syrup; stir until well combined.

2 Spoon mixture into 25 ice-cube tray holes (2-tablespoon capacity). Insert popsicle sticks; freeze for 5 hours or until set.

3 Stir shredded coconut in a small frying pan over medium heat for 5 minutes or until golden. Transfer immediately to a small bowl; cool. Stir in extra pecans until combined.

4 Carefully ease power bites from holes; dip in coconut mixture. Store in an airtight container in the freezer until ready to eat.

nutritional count per bite 7.3g total fat (1g saturated fat); 486kJ (116 cal); 10g carbohydrate; 2.3g protein; 1.2g fibre

tips Coconut butter is the blended flesh of coconut. Spirulina is a cyanobacterium (sometimes referred to as blue-green algae although this is not technically correct) that grows in lakes. It is sold as a powder or as tablets. Spirulina powder is rich in protein – a tablespoon provides 4g of protein – and contains all of the essential amino acids. It is also a very good source of iron, making it a great supplement for vegans and vegetarians. It's rich in B group vitamins, copper and manganese, and is a source of the plant omega-3 fat, alpha-linolenic acid (ALA). Coconut butter and spirulina are both available from health food stores. Bites can be stored in the freezer for up to 1 month.

ROASTED ONION SOCCA
WITH CHILLI YOGHURT

PREP + COOK TIME 40 MINUTES   SERVES 8

Socca, also known as farinata, is a traditional Italian and Provençal pancake made from chickpea flour. You will need an ovenproof frying pan for this recipe.

1 medium brown onion (150g)

½ cup (125ml) olive oil

1½ cups (180g) chickpea (besan) flour

1 teaspoon salt flakes

1¼ cups (310ml) lukewarm water

2 teaspoons chopped fresh rosemary

1 tablespoon small fresh rosemary sprigs

¼ cup (20g) finely grated parmesan

chilli yoghurt

½ cup (140g) greek-style yoghurt

1 teaspoon raw honey

1 tablespoon coarsely chopped fresh flat-leaf parsley

¼ teaspoon chilli flakes

1 Preheat oven to 200°C/400°F. Line an oven tray with baking paper.

2 Cut onion into eight wedges; separate layers. Place onion in a medium bowl with 1 tablespoon of the olive oil; toss to coat. Season. Place onion on tray; bake for 20 minutes or until browned.

3 Place chickpea flour, salt, the water, chopped rosemary and ¼ cup of the olive oil in a medium bowl; whisk until smooth. Season with cracked black pepper. Set aside for 5 minutes.

4 Make chilli yoghurt.

5 Increase oven to 250°C/480°F. Heat a large heavy-based ovenproof frying pan over a medium-high heat. Add remaining oil, heat for a few seconds, pour in batter, top with onion and rosemary sprigs. Cook for 1 minute; transfer to oven, bake for 10 minutes or until golden and socca pulls away from the side of the pan.

6 Serve socca cut into wedges, topped with parmesan and chilli yoghurt.

chilli yoghurt Combine ingredients in a small bowl.

nutritional count per serving 17.6g total fat (4.9g saturated fat); 1048kJ (250 cal); 14.7g carbohydrate; 7.2g protein; 0.4g fibre

tips Reheat socca between sheets of baking paper in a sandwich press. Store socca in an airtight container in the fridge for up to 3 days or freeze for up to 1 month.

CREAMY CARROT
& MISO DIP

PREP + COOK TIME 20 MINUTES SERVES 4

2 sheets original mountain bread (50g)

cooking oil spray

2 medium carrots (260g), chopped coarsely

1 small clove garlic, chopped

1 medium shallot (25g), chopped coarsely

2 tablespoons white (shiro) miso paste

¼ cup (60ml) avocado or vegetable oil

2 teaspoons sesame oil

2 tablespoons rice wine vinegar

1 tablespoon water

1 teaspoon black sesame seeds

1 tablespoon micro coriander (cilantro) leaves

1 Preheat oven to 200°C/400°F.

2 Place mountain bread on two oven trays, spray both sides with cooking oil; season with salt. Bake for 4 minutes or until golden and crisp. Break into large pieces.

3 Blend or process carrot, garlic, shallot, miso, oils, vinegar and the water for 30 seconds or until mixture is smooth; season to taste.

4 Serve dip sprinkled with sesame seeds and coriander, with mountain bread crisps.

nutritional count per serving 18.1g total fat (2.6g saturated fat); 966kJ (231 cal); 12.1g carbohydrate; 3.3g protein; 3.5g fibre

tips Mountain bread crisps will keep in an airtight container for up to 3 days. Dip will keep in an airtight container in the fridge for up to 3 days; stir before serving.

GREEN POWER
MINI FRITTATAS

PREP + COOK TIME 35 MINUTES   MAKES 8

2 teaspoons olive oil

1 small leek (200g), sliced thinly

½ clove garlic, crushed

3 cups (120g) firmly packed baby spinach leaves, chopped finely

5 eggs

½ cup (125ml) pouring cream

1 tablespoon finely chopped fresh mint

1 tablespoon finely chopped fresh basil

1 tablespoon finely chopped fresh dill

100g (3 ounces) goat's fetta, crumbled

1 Preheat oven to 180°C/350°F. Line 8 holes of a 12-hole (⅓ cup/80ml) muffin pan with paper cases.
2 Heat oil in a medium saucepan over medium heat; cook leek, stirring, for 3 minutes. Add garlic; cook for 2 minutes or until leek is soft. Add spinach; cook, stirring, 30 seconds or until wilted. Remove from heat. Set aside.
3 Whisk eggs, cream and herbs in a medium jug; season.
4 Divide spinach mixture into pan holes; pour in egg mixture, then top with fetta.
5 Bake frittatas for 20 minutes or until set. Leave in pan for 5 minutes before serving warm or at room temperature.

nutritional count per frittata 12g total fat (6.4g saturated fat); 586kJ (140 cal); 0.9g carbohydrate; 6.6g protein; 0.7g fibre

tip Store frittatas in an airtight container in the fridge for up to 5 days or freeze for up to 1 month.

SWEET FIX

STRAWBERRY
HALVA MOUSSE

PREP TIME 30 MINUTES (+ FREEZING & REFRIGERATION) SERVES 6

2 cups (500ml) coconut cream (see tips)

250g (8 ounces) strawberries

¼ cup (90g) raw honey

2 teaspoons vanilla extract

1 cup (280g) greek-style yoghurt

¾ cup (210g) unhulled tahini (sesame seed paste)

250g (8 ounces) strawberries, extra, sliced

⅓ cup (65g) pomegranate seeds

¼ cup (35g) pistachios, chopped

1 tablespoon sesame seeds, toasted

1 Pour coconut cream into a medium metal bowl; place in the freezer for 30 minutes or until chilled.

2 Blend or process strawberries, 1 tablespoon of the honey and half the extract until smooth.

3 Whisk chilled coconut cream with yoghurt, tahini and remaining honey and extract until thickened slightly, then swirl through the strawberry mixture.

4 Spoon mixture into six 1-cup (250ml) serving glasses. Cover; refrigerate for 2 hours or until firm.

5 Serve mousse topped with sliced strawberries, pomegranate seeds, pistachios and sesame seeds.

nutritional count per serving 43g total fat (19.6g saturated fat); 2482kJ (593 cal); 36.5g carbohydrate; 15.7g protein; 2.1g fibre

tips Use a brand of coconut cream that states it is 100% natural on the label. Coconut cream that has 'emulsifying agents' added (it will state this on the label) may cause the mousse to separate into creamy and watery layers. You can make the mousse a day ahead; store, covered, in the fridge.

WATERMELON &
LEMON TEA GRANITA

PREP TIME 20 MINUTES (+ FREEZING) SERVES 6

You need to make this recipe the day before serving.

1 lemon herbal tea bag

1 cup (250ml) boiling water

1 tablespoon stevia granules or norbu (monk fruit sugar)

500g (1 pound) seedless watermelon, chopped

1½ tablespoons lemon juice

600g (1¼ pounds) seedless watermelon, extra, sliced thinly

fennel salt

1 tablespoon sea salt flakes

1 teaspoon fennel seeds

1 teaspoon finely grated lemon rind

1 Steep the tea bag in the boiling water for 10 minutes; discard tea bag. Stir stevia into tea until dissolved.

2 Blend or process chopped watermelon until smooth. Stir in tea and juice. Pour mixture into a 2.8-litre (11-cup) shallow dish.

3 Freeze granita for 1 hour. Using a fork, break up any ice crystals. Freeze for a further 6 hours, scraping with a fork every hour or until frozen.

4 Make fennel salt.

5 Divide extra sliced watermelon among serving glasses, top with granita; sprinkle with fennel salt.

fennel salt Using a pestle and mortar, crush ingredients together.

nutritional count per serving 0.3g total fat (0g saturated fat); 134kJ (32 cal); 6.3g carbohydrate; 0.5g protein; 0.7g fibre

serving suggestion Serve with extra strips of lemon rind and micro mint leaves.

BLUEBERRY POPPY SEED CRÊPES

PREP + COOK TIME 15 MINUTES SERVES 4

½ cup (120g) mascarpone

125g (4 ounces) blueberries

2 teaspoons finely grated orange rind

½ cup (75g) wholemeal spelt flour

2 teaspoons poppy seeds

1 egg

⅔ cup (160ml) milk

2 teaspoons rice malt syrup

1 teaspoon vanilla extract

cooking oil spray

2 tablespoons rice malt syrup, extra

1 Place mascarpone, ⅓ cup of the blueberries and rind in a medium bowl; mash with a fork to combine.

2 Whisk flour, poppy seeds, egg, milk, syrup and extract in a small bowl.

3 Lightly spray a crêpe pan or heavy-based small frying pan with oil. Heat pan over medium heat; pour a scant ¼ cup of the batter into pan; swirl pan to coat base evenly. Cook crêpe for 2 minutes or until browned underneath. Turn, cook for a further 1 minute or until browned. Repeat with remaining crêpe batter to make a total of four crêpes.

4 Spread each crêpe with a slightly rounded tablespoon of mascarpone mixture; fold into triangles to enclose. Serve crêpes topped with remaining blueberries; drizzle with extra syrup. Sprinkle with strips of orange rind, if you like.

nutritional count per serving 18.4g total fat (11.2g saturated fat); 1350kJ (323 cal); 32.1g carbohydrate; 7.6g protein; 0.8g fibre

SALTED COCONUT & PASSIONFRUIT SEMIFREDDO

PREP + COOK TIME 30 MINUTES (+ FREEZING) SERVES 10

2 cups (500ml) coconut cream (see tips)

6 eggs, separated

⅓ cup (115g) raw honey or pure maple syrup

2 teaspoons vanilla extract

½ cup (50g) coconut milk powder

1 teaspoon sea salt flakes

⅓ cup (80ml) fresh passionfruit pulp

½ cup (25g) unsweetened coconut flakes

¼ cup (60ml) fresh passionfruit pulp, extra

1 tablespoon micro mint or small mint leaves

1 Pour coconut cream into a medium metal bowl; place in the freezer for 30 minutes or until chilled.

2 Grease a 9cm (3¾-inch) deep, 11.5cm x 20cm (4¾-inch x 8-inch) loaf pan. Line with baking paper, extending the paper 5cm (2-inches) over sides of pan.

3 Beat egg yolks, 2 tablespoons of the honey and extract in a small bowl with an electric mixer on high for 5 minutes or until thick and pale. Transfer to a large bowl.

4 Beat egg whites in a clean small bowl with an electric mixer until soft peaks form. Gradually add the remaining honey; beat until thick and glossy.

5 Whisk chilled coconut cream, coconut milk powder and salt in a medium bowl until slightly thickened. Gently fold egg whites and coconut cream mixture into egg yolk mixture.

6 Pour mixture into pan; freeze for 1 hour or until mixture has thickened slightly. Swirl through passionfruit pulp; freeze for at least another 3 hours or overnight.

7 Stand semifreddo at room temperature for 5 minutes before inverting onto a platter. Top with coconut flakes, extra passionfruit and mint to serve.

nutritional count per serving 17.7g total fat (14.1g saturated fat); 988kJ (236 cal); 13.5g carbohydrate; 5.6g protein; 2.5g fibre

tips Use a brand of coconut cream that states it is 100% natural on the label. Coconut cream that has 'emulsifying agents' added (it will state this on the label) may cause the semifreddo to separate into creamy and watery layers. You will need about 9 passionfruit to get the amount of pulp required. You could also peel the flesh of fresh coconut with a vegetable peeler, if you prefer, and substitute it for the coconut flakes.

COCONUT & BERRY
CHIA PUDDING

PREP TIME 15 MINUTES (+ REFRIGERATION) SERVES 6

2½ cups (625ml) coconut milk

⅓ cup (55g) white chia seeds

1 teaspoon vanilla extract

2 tablespoons raw honey or pure maple syrup

1 medium banana (200g), chopped coarsely

1 tablespoon finely grated orange rind

3 cups (300g) mixed berries (see tips)

micro mint or small mint leaves, to serve

1 Place coconut milk, seeds, extract and honey in a large bowl. Cover; refrigerate for 1 hour or overnight until thick.

2 Blend or process coconut milk mixture with banana, rind and 2 cups of the berries. Spoon into six ¾-cup (180ml) serving glasses; refrigerate for 30 minutes or until pudding has thickened.

3 Serve puddings topped with remaining berries and mint.

nutritional count per serving 24.6g total fat (19.2g saturated fat); 1418kJ (338 cal); 21.9g carbohydrate; 5g protein; 4.6g fibre

tips Use whatever combination of berries you like, including cherries. If you have one, use a Thermomix or Vitamix to achieve a very smooth pudding consistency. Puddings can be made a day ahead; store, covered, in the fridge. Top with extra berries just before serving.

EARL GREY & CHOCOLATE
VEGAN CHEESECAKE

**PREP + COOK TIME 20 MINUTES
(+ STANDING & REFRIGERATION) SERVES 10**

*You need to start this recipe the day before serving.
This vegan cheesecake is based on nuts, which provides a
wonderful, natural richness and flavour. When figs are not in
season, serve this cheesecake topped with fresh raspberries
and flaked almonds.*

4 cups (600g) raw unsalted cashews

8 earl grey tea bags

¼ cup (25g) cacao powder

1 cup (230g) fresh dates, pitted

1 cup (200g) virgin coconut oil

2 teaspoons vanilla extract

8 small figs (400g), torn in half

2 teaspoons cacao powder, extra

cheesecake base

1 cup (170g) activated buckinis (buckwheat groats)

½ cup (80g) natural almonds

⅓ cup (35g) cacao powder

1 cup (230g) fresh dates, pitted

¼ cup (50g) virgin coconut oil

2 tablespoons warm water

1 teaspoon vanilla extract

1 Place cashews and tea bags in a large bowl, cover with
cold water; stand for 24 hours.

2 Grease a 22cm (9-inch) (base measure) springform pan;
line with baking paper.

3 Make cheesecake base. Using the back of a spoon,
spread mixture evenly onto base of pan. Refrigerate for
15 minutes or until firm.

4 Drain cashews and tea bags, reserving ½ cup of the
soaking liquid. Place cashews in the bowl of a food
processor; empty tea leaves from tea bags onto cashews.
Add reserved soaking liquid, cacao, dates, oil and extract;
process until mixture is as smooth as possible. Spread
filling mixture over chilled base. Refrigerate for at least
4 hours or until firm.

5 Before serving, top cheesecake with figs and dust with
extra cacao.

cheesecake base Process buckinis, nuts and cacao powder
until finely ground. With the motor operating, add dates,
oil, the water and extract; process until well combined
and the mixture sticks together when pressed.

nutritional count per serving 59.2g total fat (30g saturated
fat); 3457kJ (825 cal); 49.6g carbohydrate; 17g protein;
6g fibre

tips Activated buckinis are buckwheat groats that have
been soaked, washed, rinsed and dehydrated. The process
is said to aid digestion. If you have one, use a high-speed
blender such as a Vitamix when making the filling, to make
the mixture very smooth. Use a hot, dry knife to slice the
cheesecake cleanly.

CACAO & DATE
CARAMEL SLICE

PREP TIME 25 MINUTES (+ REFRIGERATION & FREEZING) **MAKES** 16 PIECES

½ cup (115g) fresh dates, pitted

1 cup (130g) roasted almonds

1½ tablespoons coconut oil, melted

¼ teaspoon fine sea salt flakes

date caramel

1 cup (230g) fresh dates, pitted

½ cup (125ml) pure maple syrup

⅓ cup (95g) natural crunchy peanut butter

¼ cup (60ml) melted coconut oil

cacao topping

¼ cup (20g) raw cacao powder

¼ cup (60ml) melted coconut oil

2 teaspoons pure maple syrup

1 Line a 19cm (7¾-inch) square pan with baking paper.

2 Process dates, almonds and coconut oil until smooth. Press mixture evenly onto the base of the pan. Refrigerate for 1 hour or until set.

3 Make date caramel; spread mixture evenly over base mixture in pan. Freeze for 1 hour or until firm.

4 Make cacao topping. Working quickly, pour topping over date caramel mixture; sprinkle with salt. Refrigerate for 1 hour or until set.

5 Use a hot sharp knife to cut slice into 16 pieces.

date caramel Process ingredients for 2 minutes or until very smooth.

cacao topping Whisk ingredients in a medium bowl until smooth.

nutritional count per piece 16.2g total fat (8.8g saturated fat); 1061kJ (253 cal); 22.6g carbohydrate; 3.9g protein; 3.4g fibre

tips Make cacao topping just before you are ready to use it or it may begin to set. The slice will keep in an airtight container in the fridge for up to 1 week.

BERRY MOON ROCKS

PREP + COOK TIME 15 MINUTES (+ FREEZING) SERVES 4

250g (8 ounces) small strawberries, with stems on

175g (5½ ounces) blackberries

125g (4 ounces) raspberries

400g (12½ ounces) greek-style yoghurt

1½ tablespoons raw honey

1 vanilla bean, split lengthways, seeds scraped

⅔ cup (90g) finely chopped pistachios

1 Place all berries, separated in a single layer, on a tray; freeze for 30 minutes.

2 Combine yoghurt, honey, vanilla seeds and half the pistachios in a medium bowl. Add ½ cup of the frozen raspberries to the bowl, crush against the side of the bowl with a wooden spoon.

3 Using a toothpick, dip frozen berries, one at a time into the yoghurt mixture; place berries on a baking-paper-lined tray. Freeze for 3 hours until coating is set. Cover remaining yoghurt mixture; refrigerate.

4 Repeat dipping coated berries in remaining yoghurt mixture for a second coat; sprinkle with remaining pistachios. Freeze for 5 hours or overnight until frozen. Store in an airtight container in the freezer.

nutritional count per serving 17.6g total fat (5.2g saturated fat); 1449kJ (346 cal); 31.7g carbohydrate; 11.9g protein; 5.7g fibre

tips Swap mango or pineapple chunks for berries. Use any leftover yoghurt for breakfast or on its own as a delicious snack. Store berry moon rocks in the freezer for up to 2 weeks.

TURMERIC & HONEY TONIC

PREP + COOK TIME 15 MINUTES
SERVES 2 (MAKES 2 CUPS)

Place 2 cups unsweetened almond milk, 1 tablespoon raw honey, 2 teaspoons grated fresh turmeric, 1 cinnamon stick and 4 slices fresh ginger in a small saucepan over low-medium heat; bring almost to the boil. Remove from heat; set aside for 10 minutes to allow flavours to infuse. Strain through a fine sieve into heatproof glasses; dust with a pinch of ground cinnamon.

HOT! HOT! HOT! CHOCOLATE

PREP + COOK TIME 20 MINUTES
SERVES 2 (MAKES 3 CUPS)

Split a vanilla bean lengthways, scrape seeds, using the tip of a knife; add seeds and pod to a small saucepan. Cut 1 fresh long red chilli into four. Add three pieces to the pan; thinly slice remaining chilli, reserve to serve. Add 3 cups coconut milk blend (see tip) to the pan; bring to the boil. Remove from heat; stand 5 minutes to infuse. Discard chilli and bean. Stir 2 tablespoons raw cacao powder and 1 tablespoon rice malt syrup into infused milk; simmer, stirring, 2 minutes or until cacao is dissolved and milk heated through. Serve topped with remaining chilli.

tip We used Pureharvest Coco Quench a blend of coconut and rice milks; it has a thinner consistency than canned coconut milk, but still has a great coconut milk taste.

DRINKS

TURKISH NIGHT CAP

PREP + COOK TIME 10 MINUTES
SERVES 2 (MAKES 1½ CUPS)

Stir 2 cups milk, 1 tablespoon raw honey and 2 cinnamon sticks in a small saucepan over low-medium heat; simmer, without boiling, for 10 minutes. Remove from heat; stand for 10 minutes. Discard cinnamon. Return pan to low heat; simmer 5 minutes or until heated through. Stir in 1 teaspoon rosewater, or to taste (see tip). Pour into heatproof glasses; dust with ground cinnamon.

tip The strength of rosewater varies from brand to brand, start with a little less, then taste and adjust to your liking.

HOT SALTED CAROB LATTE

PREP + COOK TIME 10 MINUTES
SERVES 2 (MAKES 3 CUPS)

Split a vanilla bean lengthways, scrape seeds from one pod half using the tip of a knife; add seeds and pod half to a small saucepan. Add 3 cups soy milk, 1½ tablespoons carob powder, pinch of salt flakes and 1 tablespoon raw honey to pan. Place pan over low-medium heat; simmer, stirring continuously, for 5 minutes or until carob powder dissolves and mixture is heated. Discard pod. Transfer to a blender; blend until frothy. Pour into heatproof glasses; dust with ¼ teaspoon carob powder.

TAHINI CARAMEL
CHOC CUPS

PREP + COOK TIME 30 MINUTES
(+ STANDING & FREEZING) **MAKES** 12

1 cup (150g) raw cashews

3 cups (750ml) water

220g (7 ounces) dried dates, chopped coarsely

⅓ cup (45g) coconut butter

¼ cup (65g) unhulled tahini (sesame seed paste)

⅓ cup (80ml) pure maple syrup

1 teaspoon salt flakes

¼ cup (60ml) water, extra

base

220g (7 ounces) dried dates, chopped coarsely

1 cup (140g) macadamias, chopped coarsely

2 tablespoons cacao nibs

choc layer

½ cup (80g) coconut butter

½ cup (125ml) pure maple syrup

½ cup (50g) cacao powder

1 vanilla bean, split lengthways, seeds scraped

2 tablespoons hot water

1 Place cashews and the water in a medium bowl; stand for 2 hours. Drain well.

2 Grease a 12-hole (⅓-cup/80ml) muffin pan; line each hole with two strips of baking paper crossed over one another.

3 Make base; press rounded tablespoons of base mixture firmly into each pan hole. Refrigerate.

4 To make caramel, process the drained cashews, dates, coconut butter, tahini, maple syrup, salt and the extra water until smooth. Spoon rounded tablespoons of the caramel mixture equally among the bases; using wet fingers, level the surface.

5 Make choc layer. Spoon rounded teaspoons of choc layer over caramel; using a hot wet spoon, spread chocolate evenly. Freeze for 40 minutes or until firm.

6 Gently loosen cups from side of the pan holes with a hot palette knife; remove cups by lifting the baking paper strips.

base Process dates to a coarse paste. Add macadamias and cacao nibs; pulse until coarsely chopped.

choc layer Stir coconut butter and maple syrup in a small saucepan over medium heat until melted. Remove from heat. Add cacao powder, vanilla bean seeds and the hot water; whisk to combine.

nutritional count per cup 30.3g total fat (4g saturated fat); 1961kJ (469 cal); 44g carbohydrate; 6.5g protein; 4.9g fibre

tip Coconut butter is the processed flesh of coconut. It is available from health food stores.

GREEN CHILLI
MANGO & MELON SORBET

PREP + COOK TIME 10 MINUTES (+ FREEZING) SERVES 4

This refreshing sorbet uses ripe summer fruit and tooth-friendly monk fruit sugar for sweetness, but best of all you don't need an ice-cream machine to make it.

2½ cups (520g) finely chopped mango (see tips)

2½ cups (450g) finely chopped honeydew melon (see tips)

1 fresh long green chilli, seeded, chopped finely

1½ tablespoon finely chopped fresh mint

½ cup fresh micro mint leaves

sugar syrup

½ cup (125ml) pure fresh apple juice

1 tablespoon finely grated lime rind

2 tablespoons lime juice

⅓ cup (65g) norbu (monk fruit sugar)

1 Place mango and melon in a single layer on a baking-paper-lined tray; sprinkle with chilli. Cover; freeze for 5 hours or overnight.

2 Make sugar syrup.

3 Place frozen fruit, chilli and chopped mint in a food processor. With the motor running, slowly pour in sugar syrup until mixture is a smooth sorbet consistency. Tip into a deep freezer-safe tray; freeze for 3½ hours, whisking half way through to break up ice crystals.

4 Serve scoops of sorbet in chilled glasses with micro mint leaves.

sugar syrup Bring apple juice to the boil in a small saucepan. Reduce heat to medium; simmer until reduced by half. Add rind; cool to room temperature. Whisk in lime juice and norbu until dissolved.

nutritional count per serving 0.5g total fat (0.02g saturated fat); 415kJ (99 cal); 19g carbohydrate; 1.7g protein; 3.2g fibre

tips You will need about 3 medium mangoes (1.2kg) and ½ medium honeydew melon (750g) for the sorbet. You could use pineapple instead of mango. Freeze sorbet in an airtight container for up to 2 weeks. You may need to soften the sorbet for 5-10 minutes if it becomes too firm.

SALTED POPCORN
& NUT SLICE

PREP + COOK TIME 15 MINUTES (+ COOLING) MAKES 20

3 cups (45g) salted natural popped popcorn

1 cup (150g) roasted salted macadamias, chopped

1 cup (160g) roasted salted peanuts, chopped

1 cup (80g) roasted coconut chips

1½ cups (450g) raw honey

1 Line an oven tray with baking paper.

2 Combine popcorn, nuts and coconut in a medium bowl. Place honey in a frying pan over medium-high heat; bring to the boil. Reduce heat; simmer for 5 minutes or until honey starts to caramelise. (Make sure you watch the mixture, once it starts to caramelise it can quickly burn.)

3 Immediately pour honey over popcorn mixture; stir quickly to combine. Using a spatula, scrape mixture out onto the tray; cover with a piece of baking paper. Using a rolling pin, roll out flat; remove top layer of paper, leave to cool and set. Serve cut into pieces.

nutritional count per piece 11.3g total fat (2.6g saturated fat); 861kJ (206 cal); 23.3g carbohydrate; 3.1g protein; 0.3g fibre

tips You can use any kind of nuts in this recipe. This slice can be stored in an airtight container in the fridge for up to 2 weeks.

COCONUT &
MANGO POPSICLES

PREP + COOK TIME 25 MINUTES (+ FREEZING) MAKES 8

1¾ cups (265g) frozen diced mango

½ cup (125ml) pure fresh apple juice

2 tablespoons norbu (monk fruit sugar)

¼ cup (60ml) water

270ml coconut cream

½ teaspoon sea salt flakes

8 popsicle sticks

¼ cup (10g) coconut flakes, toasted

1 Process mango and apple juice until smooth. Place 2 tablespoons mango puree into each of eight ½-cup (125ml) popsicle moulds; freeze for 30 minutes.
2 Meanwhile, stir norbu and the water in a small saucepan over low heat until sugar dissolves (do not allow to simmer or boil or the mixture will crystallise). Whisk sugar syrup, coconut cream and salt to combine. Spoon mixture into popsicle moulds to fill. Cover moulds with a double layer of plastic wrap; this will help to keep the popsicle sticks upright. Pierce plastic with a small knife, then push popsicle sticks into each hole. Freeze for at least 4 hours or overnight.
3 Dip popsicle moulds briefly in boiling water; remove popsicles. Place toasted coconut in a small bowl, dip each popsicle quickly in hot water then into the coconut. Freeze on a baking-paper-lined tray for 10 minutes or until ready to eat.

nutritional count per popsicle 8.8g total fat (7.8g saturated fat); 461kJ (110 cal); 6.4g carbohydrate; 0.9g protein; 0.7g fibre

BLOOD ORANGE
FIZZED JELLY

PREP + COOK TIME 30 MINUTES
(+ STANDING & FREEZING) SERVES 6

The trick to creating these delightful fizzy jellies is to chill the glasses first and set the jellies quickly in the freezer, preserving all the bubbles.

3 cups (750ml) blood orange juice

½ cup (100g) norbu (monk fruit sugar)

2½ leaves titanium-strength gelatine (12.5g)

1¼ cups (310ml) soda water, chilled

2 tablespoons micro basil or small basil leaves

blood orange salad

4 medium blood oranges (680g)

2 pink grapefruit (700g)

100g (3 ounces) strawberries, sliced thickly

1 teaspoon shredded fresh basil leaves

1 teaspooon norbu (monk fruit sugar)

1 Chill six ½ cup (125ml) dessert glasses in the freezer.
2 Strain blood orange juice into a heavy-based medium saucepan. Add norbu; stir over medium heat until dissolved. Bring to the boil. Reduce heat; simmer, for 15 minutes or until reduced to 1⅔ cups, skimming off any foam.
3 Soak gelatine leaves in cold water for 3 minutes or until softened. Squeeze out excess water, add gelatine to reduced juice; stir until dissolved. Cool to room temperature.
4 Transfer syrup to a large jug. Add soda water, pour into chilled glasses; freeze for 1½ hours or until set. (If you are not serving jellies immediately, cover, place in the fridge.)
5 Just before serving, make blood orange salad.
6 Serve jellies topped with blood orange salad and basil.

blood orange salad Using a small knife, cut rind with the white pith away from 1 orange. Hold the orange over a bowl to catch juices, then cut between the membrane on either side of segments to release the segment into the bowl. Using your hands, squeeze remaining juice from membrane over segments. Repeat with remaining oranges and grapefruit. Add strawberries, basil and norbu to the bowl; stir to combine. Cover; refrigerate until required.

nutritional count per serving 0.6g total fat (0.1g saturated fat); 769kJ (184 cal); 37.1g carbohydrate; 4.6g protein; 4.1g fibre

tips When blood oranges are out of season use sugar-free blood orange juice (available from most supermarkets), and regular oranges for the salad. You can use 1½ tablespoons powdered gelatine instead of the leaf gelatine. Sprinkle over reduced blood orange juice in step 2; whisk to dissolve. Omit step 3. Jellies can be made the day before and will keep in the fridge for up to 4 days.

RAW CHOCOLATE
FROZEN BANANA TREATS

PREP + COOK TIME 15 MINUTES (+ FREEZING) **MAKES** 24

6 medium bananas (1.2kg)

24 mini popsicle sticks

½ cup (100g) coconut oil, melted

2 tablespoons pure maple syrup

1½ tablespoons raw honey

1 cup (100g) cacao powder

¾ cup (120g) roasted salted peanuts, chopped finely

1 Line two trays with baking paper.

2 Peel and cut bananas into 4cm (1½-inch) pieces; place standing upright on a tray. Push a popsicle stick into each banana piece; freeze for 1 hour.

3 Stir coconut oil, maple syrup and honey in a small saucepan over a low heat until almost melted. Remove from heat; continue stirring until completely melted. Sift cacao into coconut oil mixture; whisk until smooth. Transfer to a small jug.

4 Place 1½ teaspoonfuls of chopped peanuts, apart, in small piles over remaining tray. Dip three-quarters of each banana into cacao mixture; stand upright on a pile of chopped peanuts. Freeze for a further 30 minutes or until coating is set.

nutritional count per treat 7g total fat (4.3g saturated fat); 479kJ (114 cal); 10g carbohydrate; 2.8g protein; 1.1g fibre

tips You can replace the peanuts with any nut you like. Freeze these treats in an airtight container for up to 3 days.

ROSEWATER WATERMELON
SALAD WITH ROSEHIP SYRUP

PREP + COOK TIME 40 MINUTES   SERVES 4

4 rosehip and hibiscus tea bags

⅔ cup (160ml) hot water

1 tablespoon raw honey

2 tablespoons rosewater

800g (1½ pounds) piece seedless watermelon

4 medium nectarines (480g)

500g (1 pound) strawberries

⅓ cup (45g) pistachios, chopped coarsely

¼ cup loosely packed fresh mint leaves, chopped finely

1 tablespoon micro basil or small fresh mint leaves, extra

1 Place tea bags in a heatproof jug, cover with the hot water; steep for 30 minutes. Discard tea bags. Place tea with honey in a small heavy-based saucepan, bring to a simmer over medium-high heat; cook for 8 minutes or until reduced to a thick syrup. Remove from heat; stir in rosewater, cool.

2 Meanwhile, remove rind from watermelon and cut flesh into small wedges. Halve and remove stones from nectarines; slice thinly. Halve strawberries.

3 Place chopped fruit in a large bowl with ¼ cup of the pistachios and the chopped mint; toss gently to combine. Drizzle with rosehip syrup; serve topped with remaining pistachios and extra mint.

nutritional count per serving 6.5g total fat (0.8g saturated fat); 955kJ (228 cal); 32g carbohydrate; 6g protein; 6.6g fibre

APRICOT & PISTACHIO
FROZEN YOGHURT

PREP + COOK TIME 1 HOUR
(+ COOLING & FREEZING) SERVES 4

1 cup (150g) dried apricots

2¼ cups (560ml) pure fresh apple juice

1 teaspoon ground cardamom

2¼ cups (630g) greek-style yoghurt

¼ cup (90g) raw honey

2 tablespoons sesame seeds, toasted

½ cup (70g) pistachios, chopped coarsely

1 Place apricots and juice in a medium frying pan; bring to the boil. Reduce heat; simmer for 15 minutes or until apricots are tender and plump and the apple juice is syrupy. Cool.

2 Process cooled apricot mixture with cardamom until smooth. Transfer mixture to a large bowl. Cover; refrigerate until required.

3 Combine yoghurt, honey, sesame seeds and half the pistachios in a medium bowl. Place mixture in an ice-cream machine (see tips). Following manufacturer's directions, churn on the frozen yoghurt setting for 40 minutes until frozen. Spoon frozen yoghurt into the bowl with apricot mixture; fold the two mixtures together gently to create a marbled effect. Spoon into a 1.25-litre (5-cup) loaf pan, cover, freeze for 5 hours or overnight.

4 Serve yoghurt topped with remaining pistachios.

nutritional count per serving 21.6g total fat (7.5g saturated fat); 2550kJ (609 cal); 88.4g carbohydrate; 15.8g protein; 8.2g fibre

tips If you don't have an ice-cream machine, place yoghurt mixture only in the loaf pan, then cover with foil; freeze for 1 hour or until half frozen. Pulse mixture in a food processor to break-up ice crystals. Return to pan, cover with foil; repeat freezing and processing. Fold through apricot mixture, return to pan and cover with foil; freeze for 5 hours or overnight until frozen. Store yogurt in the freezer for up to 2 weeks.

RAW CHOCOLATE
POWER PUFFS

PREP + COOK TIME 20 MINUTES (+ STANDING) **MAKES** 36

1¼ cups (25g) puffed rice

1¼ cups (40g) puffed millet

½ cup (75g) sunflower seeds

¾ cup (90g) goji berries or unsweetened
dried cranberries

¼ cup (35g) chia seeds

½ cup (100g) coconut oil, melted

½ cup (180g) raw honey

1¼ cups (125g) cacao powder

1 Combine puffed rice, puffed millet, sunflower seeds, goji berries and chia seeds in a large bowl.

2 Stir coconut oil and honey in a small saucepan over low heat until almost melted; remove from heat. Add cacao; whisk to combine. Pour cacao mixture over dry ingredients in bowl; stir well to combine.

3 Line an oven tray with baking paper. Using wet hands, roll heaped tablespoons of mixture into balls, place on tray; refrigerate for 30 minutes. Place in an airtight container until ready to eat.

nutritional count per puff 4.8g total fat (2.9g saturated fat); 335kJ (80 cal); 7.4g carbohydrate; 2g protein; 0.7g fibre

SQUASHED PLUM & RICOTTA SANDWICHES

PREP + COOK TIME 15 MINUTES SERVES 4

2 tablespoons melted coconut oil

2 teaspoons sugar-free icing mix (see tip)

1 teaspoon ground ginger

4 medium blood plums (340g), halved, stones removed

1 tablespoon pure maple syrup

8 x 2cm (¾-inch) slices sourdough bread

1 cup (240g) firm ricotta

1 Preheat a sandwich press. Brush press with half the coconut oil.

2 Combine icing mix and ginger in a small bowl.

3 Place plums, cut-side down, in the sandwich press. Cook, pressing down on the lid occasionally, for 6 minutes or until plums are tender and browned. Remove plums; wipe sandwich press clean.

4 Meanwhile, combine maple syrup and remaining coconut oil in a small bowl. Brush oil mixture over one side of each piece of bread.

5 Place four slices of bread, oiled-side down, on a board; spread with ricotta and top with plums. Top with remaining bread slices, oiled-side up. Cook in sandwich press, in two batches, for 3 minutes or until golden and heated through. Serve dusted with ginger mixture.

nutritional count per serving 17.3g total fat (13g saturated fat); 1565kJ (374 cal); 39g carbohydrate; 13g protein; 3.9g fibre

tip We used Natvia icing mix made from stevia. It is available in the baking aisle from most supermarkets.

BUCKWHEAT WAFFLES
WITH GRILLED PEACHES

PREP + COOK TIME 15 MINUTES SERVES 4

⅓ cup (60g) coconut oil

2 tablespoons norbu (monk fruit sugar)

3 eggs, separated

1 cup (150g) self-raising flour

⅓ cup (50g) plain (all-purpose) flour

⅓ cup (50g) buckwheat flour

⅓ cup (50g) cornflour (cornstarch)

1 teaspoon baking powder

1 teaspoon bicarbonate of soda (baking soda)

½ teaspoon salt

½ teaspoon ground ginger

1½ cups (375ml) milk

1½ teaspoons white vinegar

cooking oil spray

4 medium yellow peaches (600g), halved, stones removed

1 cup (280g) greek-style yoghurt

⅓ cup small fresh mint leaves

⅓ cup (90g) raw honey

1 Beat coconut oil and norbu in a medium bowl with an electric mixer until combined. Beat in egg yolks one at a time.

2 Beat egg whites in a small bowl with an electric mixer until soft peaks form. Gently fold egg whites into egg-yolk mixture.

3 Fold sifted dry ingredients, milk and vinegar into egg mixture until mixture just comes together (do not over mix; it may look quite lumpy at this stage).

4 Spray a heated waffle iron with cooking oil; pour a level ½-cup of batter on the bottom element of waffle iron. Close iron; cook waffle 2 minutes or until browned on both sides and crisp. Transfer to a plate; cover to keep warm. Repeat to make 8 waffles in total.

5 Meanwhile, heat an oiled chargrill pan over high heat; cook peaches for 3 minutes each side or until grill marks show.

6 Serve waffles with yoghurt, peach halves and mint; drizzle with honey.

nutritional count per serving 26g total fat (18.8g saturated fat); 3014kJ (520 cal); 99.4g carbohydrate; 18.4g protein; 4g fibre

BAKING

CACAO & HAZELNUT
COOKIES

PREP + COOK TIME 30 MINUTES MAKES 18

½ cup (80g) firmly packed fresh dates, pitted

2 cups (200g) ground hazelnuts

1½ cups (225g) wholemeal spelt flour

¼ cup (50g) chia seeds

1 teaspoon ground cinnamon

pinch sea salt flakes

¼ cup (50g) virgin coconut oil, at room temperature

½ cup (170g) rice malt syrup

1 egg

2 teaspoons vanilla extract

½ cup (50g) cacao nibs

1 Preheat oven to 160°C/325°F. Line two oven trays with baking paper.

2 Place dates in a small heatproof bowl, cover with boiling water; stand for 5 minutes. Drain.

3 Process dates, ground hazelnuts, flour, seeds, cinnamon, salt, oil, syrup, egg and extract until well combined. Stir in cacao nibs.

4 Using damp hands, roll 2-tablespoonfuls of mixture into a ball, place on tray; flatten with the palm of your hand into a 4cm (1½-inch) round. Using the back of a damp fork, mark each cookie.

5 Bake cookies for 15 minutes or until a cookie can gently be pushed without breaking. Cool on trays.

nutritional count per cookie 12.5g total fat (3.1g saturated fat); 890kJ (213 cal); 19.6g carbohydrate; 4.7g protein; 2.3g fibre

tip Cacao nibs are created in the early stages of chocolate production; cocoa beans are dried then roasted, after which they are crushed into what is termed 'nibs'. The nibs are then ground to separate the cocoa butter and cocoa solids. Nibs are both textural and chocolatey with no sweetness. Buy from health food stores and specialist food stores.

CINNAMON & FIG
BAKED APPLES

PREP + COOK TIME 40 MINUTES SERVES 6

¼ cup (35g) roasted hazelnuts, skins removed

3 dried figs

6 pitted prunes

½ teaspoon ground cinnamon

1 teaspoon vanilla extract

6 large red apples (1.2kg), cored (see tip)

ricotta cream

1 cup (240g) fresh firm ricotta

½ cup (125ml) milk

1 teaspoon vanilla extract

½ teaspoon finely grated mandarin rind

maple sauce

2 large mandarins (500g)

¼ cup (60ml) pure maple syrup

30g (1 ounce) cold butter, chopped finely

1 Preheat oven to 160°C/325°F. Line an oven tray with baking paper.
2 Process hazelnuts, figs, prunes, cinnamon and extract until coarsely chopped.
3 Using a small, sharp knife, score around the centre of each apple. Press hazelnut mixture into the cavities of each apple; place apples upright on tray. Bake for 30 minutes or until apples are tender.
4 Meanwhile, make ricotta cream. Make maple sauce.
5 Serve apples with ricotta cream and maple sauce.

ricotta cream Process ricotta, milk and extract until smooth; stir in rind.

maple sauce Squeeze juice from mandarins; you will need ⅔ cup. Place juice and maple syrup in a small saucepan over medium heat; simmer until reduced by half and mixture is syrupy. Remove pan from heat; whisk in butter a few pieces at a time, until melted and combined.

nutritional count per serving 13.2g total fat (6.4g saturated fat); 1683kJ (402 cal); 61g carbohydrate; 7.9g protein; 5.6g fibre

tip We used royal gala apples in this recipe.

FLOURLESS ALMOND, PLUM & ORANGE BLOSSOM LOAF

PREP + COOK TIME 1 HOURS 45 MINUTES SERVES 6

2 medium green apples (300g), grated coarsely

2 eggs, beaten lightly

¼ cup (60ml) unsweetened almond milk

2 tablespoons raw honey or pure maple syrup

2 teaspoons vanilla extract

1 teaspoon orange blossom water

2 cups (240g) ground almonds

2 teaspoons gluten-free baking powder

5 small plums (375g), halved

2 teaspoons raw honey or pure maple syrup, extra

2 tablespoons flaked coconut, toasted

1 Preheat oven to 160°C/325°F. Lightly grease a 10.5cm x 21cm x 6cm (4-inch x 8½-inch x 2½-inch) (base measure) loaf pan; line base and long sides with baking paper.

2 Combine apple, egg, almond milk, honey, extract and orange blossom water in a large bowl. Add ground almonds and baking powder; stir until just combined.

3 Spread mixture into pan, level surface; top with plums, cut-side up, pressing them slightly into the batter. Drizzle with extra honey.

4 Bake for 1½ hours or until a skewer inserted into the centre comes out clean. Top with coconut and serve warm.

nutritional count per serving 26.3g total fat (3.1g saturated fat); 1535kJ (366 cal); 19.7g carbohydrate; 11.2g protein; 5.7g fibre

tips You can also make this loaf with other stone fruit such as small peaches or apricots. You may need to cover the loaf loosely with baking paper during the last 10 minutes of baking to prevent overbrowning.

APRICOT & CARDAMOM
MUESLI SLICE

PREP + COOK TIME 40 MINUTES MAKES 18

1 cup (150g) dried apricots

2 cups (185g) quinoa flakes

½ cup (70g) quinoa flour

½ cup (75g) sunflower seeds

½ cup (80g) coarsely chopped raw almonds

1 teaspoon ground cardamom

1 teaspoon gluten-free baking powder

1 tablespoon finely grated orange rind

⅓ cup (70g) virgin coconut oil

⅓ cup (115g) raw honey

3 eggs, beaten lightly

2 teaspoons vanilla extract

2 tablespoons sugar-free apricot jam, melted, strained

1 Preheat oven to 160°C/325°F. Grease a 16cm x 26cm x 4cm (6½-inch x 10½-inch x 1½-inch) slice pan; line base and long sides with baking paper.

2 Roughly chop half the apricots; place in a large bowl. Cut remaining apricots in half lengthways; set aside.

3 Add quinoa flakes and flour, sunflower seeds, almonds, cardamom, baking powder and rind to chopped apricots in bowl; stir to combine.

4 Place coconut oil and honey in a small saucepan over medium heat; bring to the boil, stirring until melted and well combined. Pour hot mixture over dry ingredients, add eggs and extract; mix well to combine.

5 Spread mixture into pan; level the mixture with the back of a spoon. Top with apricot halves, pressing down lightly into the mixture.

6 Bake slice for 20 minutes or until golden and a skewer inserted into the centre comes out clean. Brush hot slice with apricot jam; cool in the pan. Cut into pieces to serve.

nutritional count per piece 10.1g total fat (4.2g saturated fat); 803kJ (192 cal); 20g carbohydrate; 5.1g protein; 1.4g fibre

tip You can use walnuts, pecans, macadamias or cashews instead of almonds, if you like.

BANANA & COFFEE CAKE
WITH CARAMEL SAUCE

PREP + COOK TIME 1 HOUR 45 MINUTES SERVES 12

185g (6 ounces) butter, softened, chopped

1 cup (245g) granulated stevia

3 eggs

2¼ cups (335g) self-raising flour

¼ teaspoon salt

¾ teaspoon bicarbonate of soda (baking soda)

1½ teaspoons ground cinnamon

2 cups (525g) mashed ripe banana

2 teaspoons vanilla extract

¾ cup (200g) sour cream

1 cup (100g) walnut halves, roasted, chopped

¼ cup (60ml) boiling water

3 teaspoons espresso coffee granules

caramel sauce

⅔ cup (200g) rice malt syrup

125g (4 ounces) butter, softened, chopped

⅓ cup (80ml) thickened cream

1 Preheat oven to 180°C/350°F. Grease and line a deep 22cm (9-inch) round cake pan with baking paper.
2 Beat butter and stevia in a small bowl with an electric mixer until pale and fluffy. Beat in eggs, one at a time, until just combined. Transfer mixture to a large bowl. Stir sifted dry ingredients, banana, extract, sour cream, walnuts and combined water and coffee into butter mixture. Spread mixture into pan.
3 Bake cake for 1¼ hours or until a skewer inserted into the centre comes out clean. Leave cake in pan for 5 minutes before turning, top-side up, onto a wire rack to cool.
4 Meanwhile, make caramel sauce.
5 Serve cake with caramel sauce.

caramel sauce Place syrup in a small saucepan over medium heat, bring to the boil; boil for 12 minutes or until slightly darker in colour, golden and surface is covered with bubbles. Immediately add butter and cream; stir until mixture is smooth.

nutritional count per serving 37.2g total fat (20g saturated fat); 2235kJ (532 cal); 61.9g carbohydrate; 7g protein; 2.9g fibre

tips You will need about 4½ bananas to make 1½ cups mashed banana. The cake can be made a day ahead; store in an airtight container at room temperature in a cool place.

OLIVE OIL
MARMALADE CAKE

PREP + COOK TIME 1 HOUR 15 MINUTES (+ STANDING) SERVES 12

⅔ cup (160ml) extra virgin olive oil

1 cup (285g) cane-sugar-free marmalade

3 eggs

1 cup (120g) ground almonds

⅔ cup (100g) plain (all-purpose) flour

3 teaspoons baking powder

¼ cup (60ml) orange juice

orange syrup

1 medium orange (240g)

⅔ cup (160ml) orange juice

¼ cup (60ml) water

¼ cup (85g) rice malt syrup

1 cinnamon stick

3 whole cloves

1 Preheat oven to 170°C/340°F. Grease and line a deep 20cm (8-inch) round cake pan with baking paper.

2 Beat oil and marmalade in a medium bowl with an electric mixer until pale and fluffy. Beat in eggs, one at a time.

3 Sift ground almonds, flour and baking powder into a large bowl. Add almond mixture and juice to marmalade mixture; beat on low speed until just combined. Spread mixture into pan.

4 Bake cake for 55 minutes or until a skewer inserted into the centre comes out clean. Leave cake in pan for 30 minutes before turning, top-side up, onto a wire rack.

5 Meanwhile, make orange syrup.

6 Pierce the top of the cake randomly with a cake skewer. Slowly pour the warm syrup and spices over the cake, allowing the syrup to be absorbed into cake. Serve warm or at room temperature.

orange syrup Using a vegetable peeler, thinly peel rind from orange, with as little white pith as is possible; cut rind into thin strips. Place rind and remaining ingredients in a small saucepan; bring to the boil. Reduce heat; simmer for 15 minutes or until syrup thickens slightly. Remove from heat; cool syrup for 10 minutes. Remove cinnamon stick and cloves.

nutritional count per serving 20.3g total fat (2.8g saturated fat); 1113kJ (266 cal); 15.4g carbohydrate; 5.2g protein; 2.3g fibre

CHOCOLATE
HAZELNUT BROWNIES

PREP + COOK TIME 45 MINUTES **MAKES** 24

1 cup (340g) rice malt syrup

1 cup (140g) dried pitted dates, chopped coarsely

¼ teaspoon sea salt flakes

½ cup (125ml) water

½ teaspoon bicarbonate of soda (baking soda)

200g (6½ ounces) butter, chopped

3 eggs

¾ cup (75g) cocoa powder

¾ cup (75g) ground hazelnuts

½ cup (75g) buckwheat flour

½ cup (120g) sour cream

½ cup (70g) whole roasted skinless hazelnuts, halved

1½ teaspoons cocoa powder, extra

1 Preheat oven to 180°C/350°F. Grease a 20cm x 30cm (8-inch x 12-inch) slice pan; line base with baking paper, extending the paper 5cm (2-inches) over long sides.

2 Place syrup, dates, salt and the water in a small saucepan over low heat; simmer for 5 minutes or until dates are soft.

3 Stir soda into date mixture; transfer to a food processor, process until smooth. Return date mixture to pan; add butter, stir over medium heat until butter melts. Transfer mixture to a large bowl; cool for 5 minutes.

4 Whisk in eggs, one at a time. Stir in sifted cocoa, ground hazelnuts, flour, sour cream and chopped hazelnuts. Spread mixture into pan; level surface.

5 Bake brownie for 30 minutes or until a skewer inserted into the centre comes out with moist crumbs attached. Cool in pan before dusting with extra cocoa and cutting into pieces.

nutritional count per piece 13.3g total fat (6.2g saturated fat); 861kJ (205 cal); 19.5g carbohydrate; 2.6g protein; 1.5g fibre

tip Despite its name, buckwheat is unrelated to wheat and is known as a seed or pseudo-cereal, making it safe for those on coeliac diets. It is also high in fibre and protein.

CARROT CAKES WITH
DATE CREAM CHEESE FROSTING

PREP + COOK TIME 1 HOUR 45 MINUTES
(+ STANDING) SERVES 12

⅓ cup (35g) sultanas

¼ cup (60ml) boiling water

2 free-range eggs

¾ cup (185g) powdered stevia

¼ cup (85g) rice malt syrup

⅔ cup (140g) virgin coconut oil, melted

2 teaspoons vanilla extract

2 cups (340g) firmly packed coarsely grated carrot

½ cup (60g) chopped pecans, roasted

1⅔ cups (250g) self-raising flour

½ teaspoon bicarbonate of soda (baking soda)

1 teaspoon ground allspice

3 teaspoons ground cinnamon

1 teaspoon ground ginger

date cream cheese frosting

125g (4 ounces) dried pitted dates, chopped finely

2 tablespoons boiling water

250g (8 ounces) cream cheese, softened

125g (4 ounces) butter, softened

1 Preheat oven to 180°C/350°F. Grease a 6-hole (¾-cup/180ml) texas muffin pan.

2 Place sultanas in a small heatproof bowl, pour over the boiling water; stand for 10 minutes.

3 Meanwhile, whisk eggs, stevia, syrup, coconut oil and extract in a small bowl with an electric mixer for 5 minutes. Transfer mixture to a large bowl; stir in carrot, sultanas and soaking liquid, then pecans and sifted dry ingredients. Spoon mixture evenly into muffin pan holes.

4 Bake cakes for 35 minutes or until a skewer inserted into the centre of one cake comes out clean. Leave in pan for 5 minutes before turning, top-side up, onto a wire rack to cool.

5 Make date cream cheese frosting; spread on cakes.

date cream cheese frosting Process dates and the boiling water until almost smooth, scraping down the side of the bowl. Add cream cheese and butter; process, scraping down the side of the bowl, until frosting is light and fluffy.

nutritional count per cake 32g total fat (21.4g saturated fat); 1882kJ (449 cal); 48.1g carbohydrate; 6.1g protein; 1.9g fibre

tips You need about 2½ medium carrots to make 2 cups grated carrot. You could also cook the cake recipe as a slice using a 20cm x 30cm x 3cm (8-inch x 12-inch x 1¼-inch) slice pan. Line the base with baking paper, extending the paper 5cm (2-inches) over the long sides; bake 25 minutes.

ROSEMARY, LABNE & ORANGE TART

PREP + COOK TIME 1 HOUR 30 MINUTES (+ REFRIGERATION & COOLING) SERVES 8

You need to start the recipe the day before.

800g (1½ pounds) greek-style yoghurt

3 eggs

2 tablespoons raw honey

1 teaspoon vanilla extract

2 teaspoons finely chopped fresh rosemary leaves

2 cups (500ml) clear pure apple juice

1 sprig fresh rosemary, extra

3 small oranges (540g), sliced thinly

amaranth pastry

1½ cups (225g) fine amaranth flour

2 tablespoons arrowroot starch

pinch salt

⅓ cup (70g) virgin coconut oil

½ cup (125ml) ice-cold water

1 To make labne, line a medium sieve with a piece of muslin (or a clean loosely-woven cotton cloth); place sieve over a large bowl. Spoon yoghurt into muslin, cover bowl and sieve with plastic wrap; refrigerate overnight.

2 Make amaranth pastry.

3 Grease an 11cm x 34cm (4½-inch x 14-inch) rectangular loose-based fluted tart pan. Roll pastry between sheets of baking paper until 3mm (⅛-inch) thick. Lift pastry into pan, press into base and sides; trim excess pastry. Prick base all over with a fork. Cover, refrigerate for 30 minutes.

4 Preheat oven to 200°C/400°F.

5 Place tart pan on an oven tray; line with baking paper, fill with dried beans or rice. Bake for 15 minutes. Remove paper and beans; bake a further 5 minutes or until browned lightly. Cool.

6 Reduce oven temperature to 140°C/285°F.

7 Drain labne; whisk in a large bowl with eggs, honey, extract and chopped rosemary. Spoon into cooled pastry case. Bake for 25 minutes or until just set. Cool to room temperature. Refrigerate until cold.

8 Meanwhile, place apple juice and extra rosemary in a medium saucepan; bring to the boil over medium heat. Add orange slices to pan, reduce heat to low; simmer for 15 minutes or until tender; cool.

9 Just before serving, drain orange slices and arrange over the cooled tart.

amaranth pastry Process flour, starch, salt and coconut oil until combined. With the motor operating, gradually add the iced water in a thin steady stream until a dough forms. Flatten pastry into a disc, wrap in plastic wrap; refrigerate for 30 minutes.

nutritional count per serving 18.4g total fat (13g saturated fat); 1719kJ (410 cal); 49.3g carbohydrate; 11.4g protein; 5.4g fibre

tip If you like, make the whole tart a day ahead and store in the fridge. Top with the oranges just before serving.

COCONUT & VANILLA MUFFINS

PREP + COOK TIME 40 MINUTES MAKES 12

Preheat oven to 180°C/350°F. Line a 12-hole (⅓ cup/80ml) muffin pan with paper cases. Sift 2 cups spelt flour and 2 teaspoons baking powder into a medium bowl. Whisk 1 teaspoon vanilla extract (see tip), 1 cup yoghurt, ½ cup melted cooled virgin coconut oil, ½ cup pure maple syrup and 2 eggs in a medium jug. Pour over dry ingredients; stir with a fork to just combine. Spoon mixture into cases; top with 1 cup coconut flakes. Bake for 30 minutes or until a skewer inserted into the centre comes out clean.

tip Vanilla extract contains a tiny amount of refined sugar; if you prefer, either use the scraped seeds of a vanilla bean or vanilla bean powder available from health food stores.

PEACH & GINGER CRUMBLE MUFFINS

PREP + COOK TIME 40 MINUTES MAKES 12

Preheat oven to 180°C/350°F. Line a 12-hole (⅓ cup/80ml) muffin pan with paper cases. Sift 2 cups spelt flour, 2 teaspoons baking powder, 1½ teaspoons ground ginger and 1 teaspoon ground cinnamon into a medium bowl; stir in 2 coarsely chopped small (250g) peaches. Whisk 1 teaspoon vanilla extract (see previous tip), 1 cup yoghurt, ½ cup melted cooled virgin coconut oil, ½ cup pure maple syrup and 2 eggs in a medium jug. Pour over dry ingredients; stir with a fork to just combine. Spoon mixture into cases. Place ⅓ cup coconut sugar, ½ cup spelt flour and 1 teaspoon ground cinnamon in a small bowl; rub in 60g (2oz) chopped cold unsalted butter until mixture resembles coarse crumbs. Sprinkle crumble on muffins. Bake for 30 minutes or until a skewer inserted into the centre comes out clean.

LEMON, THYME & FETTA MUFFINS

PREP + COOK TIME 40 MINUTES MAKES 12

Preheat oven to 180°C/350°F. Line a 12-hole (⅓ cup/80ml) muffin pan with paper cases. Sift 2 cups spelt flour and 2 teaspoons baking powder into a medium bowl; stir in 2 teaspoons finely grated lemon rind and 1 tablespoon finely chopped fresh thyme. Whisk 1¼ cups yoghurt, ½ cup melted cooled virgin coconut oil, ¼ cup pure maple syrup and 2 eggs in a medium jug. Pour over dry ingredients; stir with a fork until almost combined. Fold through ½ cup crumbled goat's fetta. Spoon mixture into cases; top with combined ⅔ cup crumbled goat's fetta, ⅓ cup pepitas and 2 tablespoons fresh thyme leaves. Bake for 30 minutes or until a skewer inserted into the centre comes out clean.

CHOC, BEETROOT & WALNUT MUFFINS

PREP + COOK TIME 40 MINUTES MAKES 12

Preheat oven to 180°C/350°F. Line a 12-hole (⅓ cup/80ml) muffin pan with paper cases. Sift 2 cups spelt flour, ⅓ cup cacao powder and 2½ teaspoons baking powder into a medium bowl. Coarsely grate 1 medium (130g) washed, unpeeled beetroot, place in a large jug. Add 1½ cups yoghurt, ½ cup melted cooled virgin coconut oil, ½ cup pure maple syrup and 2 eggs to the jug; whisk with a fork to combine. Pour over dry ingredients; stir with the fork until almost combined. Fold in 8 pitted and coarsely chopped fresh medjool dates and ½ cup chopped roasted walnuts. Spoon mixture into cases. Bake for 30 minutes or until a skewer inserted into the centre comes out clean.

MUFFINS

GINGER, PEAR & PISTACHIO CRUMBLES

PREP + COOK TIME 1 HOUR 30 MINUTES   SERVES 6

6 medium firm pears (1.4kg), peeled, chopped coarsely

125g (4 ounces) fresh or frozen raspberries

2 tablespoons cornflour (cornstarch) or arrowroot

1 tablespoon finely grated fresh ginger

¼ cup (60ml) pure maple syrup

1 tablespoon lemon juice

1 teaspoon vanilla extract

1 cup (140g) pistachios

1 cup (120g) pecans

1 cup (90g) rolled oats

¼ cup (60ml) olive oil

¼ cup (60ml) pure maple syrup, extra

1 teaspoon vanilla extract, extra

2 tablespoons freeze-dried or fresh pomegranate seeds

2 cups (560g) thick no-sugar-added vanilla yoghurt (see tips)

1 Preheat oven to 160°C/325°F.

2 Place pears, raspberries, cornflour, ginger, syrup, juice and extract in a large bowl; toss to coat fruit in mixture. Spoon mixture into six 1-cup (250ml) ovenproof dishes.

3 Process pistachios and pecans until chopped roughly. Transfer to a medium bowl; stir in oats, oil and extra syrup and extract; spoon over fruit mixture.

4 Bake crumbles, uncovered, for 1 hour. Cover with foil; bake a further 15 minutes or until crumble topping is golden and pears are soft.

5 Just before serving, sprinkle pomegranate seeds on crumbles, serve with yoghurt.

nutritional count per serving 42.3g total fat (7.5g saturated fat); 3130kJ (747 cal); 73.6g carbohydrate; 13.9g protein; 8g fibre

tips If you can't find sugar-free vanilla yoghurt you can stir vanilla bean seeds or extract through greek-style yoghurt. Freeze-dried pomegranate seeds are available from health food stores or use unsweetened dried cranberries instead.

RASPBERRY, POLENTA &
PINK PEPPERCORN SCROLLS

PREP + COOK TIME 45 MINUTES MAKES 8

2 cups (300g) white spelt flour, plus extra, for dusting

½ cup (85g) fine polenta

1½ teaspoons baking powder

pinch salt

½ cup (125ml) buttermilk

¼ cup (85g) rice malt syrup

1 teaspoon pink peppercorns

1 teaspoon vanilla extract

1 tablespoon finely grated orange rind

2 tablespoons rice malt syrup, extra

75g (2½ ounces) fresh raspberries

1 Preheat oven to 180°C/350°F. Grease an oven tray; line with baking paper.

2 Combine flour, polenta, baking powder and salt in a large bowl. Make a well in the centre. Add buttermilk and syrup. Using a butter knife, 'cut' through the mixture until a rough dough forms.

3 Using a mortar and pestle, crush pink peppercorns. Stir in extract, rind and 1 tablespoon of the extra syrup.

4 Turn dough onto a lightly floured surface; knead lightly. Press out into a 18cm x 28cm (7¼-inch x 11¼-inch) rectangle; spread with peppercorn mixture. Using your hands, tear raspberries into small pieces, place on dough.

5 Starting from one long side, roll up dough to form a log. Cut log into 8 slices. Place slices 5cm (2-inches) apart, cut-side up, on tray.

6 Bake scrolls for 25 minutes or until risen and light golden. Brush with remaining extra syrup. Serve warm.

nutritional count per scroll 1.5g total fat (0.4g saturated fat); 1155kJ (276 cal); 58g carbohydrate; 7.2g protein; 1.4g fibre

tips Pink peppercorns are unrelated to black peppercorns, they carry no heat and have a pine-like taste slightly similar to juniper berries. If unavailable don't worry, the recipe will still have plenty of flavour without them. The scrolls are best eaten warm on the day of making. If made ahead on the day, reheat in the oven before serving.

MAPLE GINGERBREAD MUFFINS
WITH KUMARA BUTTER

PREP + COOK TIME 1 HOUR (+ REFRIGERATION) MAKES 12

1¾ cups (265g) wholemeal spelt flour

⅓ cup (40g) ground almonds

2 tablespoons ground ginger

1 teaspoon mixed spice

1½ teaspoons baking powder

¼ teaspoon bicarbonate of soda (baking soda)

3 eggs

⅓ cup (80ml) olive oil

⅓ cup (80ml) pure maple syrup

¾ cup (180ml) unsweetened almond milk

1 teaspoon vanilla extract

kumara butter

400g (12½ ounces) kumara (orange sweet potato), chopped coarsely

¼ cup (50g) virgin coconut oil

1 teaspoon vanilla extract

pinch sea salt

1 Make kumara butter.

2 Preheat oven to 160°C/325°F. Grease a 12-hole (⅓-cup/80ml) muffin pan. Cut 12 x 12cm (4¾-inch) squares of baking paper, fold into quarters, then open out again.

3 Sift flour, ground almonds, ginger, mixed spice, baking powder and soda in a large bowl. Whisk eggs, oil, syrup, almond milk and extract in a medium bowl until combined. Add to the dry ingredients; mix until just combined.

4 Working with one square of baking paper at a time, place in a muffin hole; pour in one-twelfth of the batter. Repeat with the remaining baking paper squares and batter.

5 Bake muffins for 15 minutes or until a skewer inserted into the centre comes out clean. Serve muffins warm with kumara butter.

kumara butter Place kumara in a small saucepan with just enough water to cover. Bring to the boil; boil for 12 minutes or until kumara is tender. Drain; return to pan, mash until smooth. Stir in coconut oil, extract and salt. Spoon into a small bowl, cover with plastic wrap; refrigerate until firm.

nutritional count per muffin 15.6g total fat (5.5g saturated fat); 1142kJ (273 cal); 25.4g carbohydrate; 6.8g protein; 1.4g fibre

tips These muffins are best made on the day of serving. You could line the muffin pan with standard paper cases.

GLAZED FIG & WHOLE
ORANGE CAKES

PREP + COOK TIME 3 HOURS 20 MINUTES (+ STANDING) MAKES 12

6 dried figs (135g), halved

1½ cups (375ml) fresh pure apple juice

2 medium oranges (480g), washed

1⅔ cups (250g) coconut sugar

5 eggs

2¾ cups (280g) ground almonds

1 teaspoon baking powder

¼ cup (20g) flaked almonds

1 Place figs and juice in a medium saucepan; soak for 2 hours. Remove figs with a slotted spoon; reserve juice in pan.

2 Fill another medium saucepan two-thirds with water, add whole oranges; bring to the boil. Reduce heat to a simmer. Cover oranges with the lid from a smaller saucepan to keep submerged; simmer for 2 hours, topping up with water if necessary to keep oranges submerged. Drain; cool to room temperature.

3 Preheat oven to 180°C/350°F. Line a 12-hole (⅓ cup/80ml) muffin pan with paper cases.

4 Cut oranges in half, discard any seeds. Process oranges (rind and flesh) until smooth. Add coconut sugar, eggs, ground almonds and baking powder to the food processor, pulse until well combined. Spoon mixture into paper cases; place a fig, cut-side up, on top; sprinkle with almonds.

5 Bake cakes for 1 hour or until a skewer inserted in the centre comes out clean.

6 Meanwhile, simmer saucepan with apple juice over medium heat for 8 minutes or until syrupy.

7 Brush syrup over warm cakes. Serve topped with greek-style yoghurt, if you like.

nutritional count per cake 16g total fat (1.5g saturated fat); 1331kJ (318 cal); 34g carbohydrate; 8.8g protein; 5.5g fibre

tips You can use mandarins instead of oranges, if you like. If you find the cakes are getting too brown, cover with foil during cooking.

ZUCCHINI, PARMESAN & ROSEMARY CRACKERS

PREP + COOK TIME 30 MINUTES   MAKES 35

60g (2 ounces) pepitas (pumpkin seeds)

½ cup (55g) coarsely chopped walnuts

1 small zucchini (90g), chopped coarsely

⅓ cup (25g) finely grated parmesan

1 tablespoon linseeds (flaxseeds)

1 tablespoon sesame seeds

1 tablespoon poppy seeds

½ teaspoon cumin seeds

½ teaspoon dried oregano

1 teaspoon finely chopped fresh rosemary

1 tablespoon fresh rosemary leaves, extra

½ teaspoon sea salt flakes

1 Preheat oven to 180°C/350°F.

2 Process pepitas and walnuts until finely ground. Add zucchini; process to combine. Add parmesan, linseeds, sesame seeds, poppy seeds, cumin seeds, oregano and finely chopped rosemary; pulse to combine. Season.

3 Spread mixture onto a piece of baking paper; top with a second sheet of baking paper. Roll into a 25cm x 35cm (10-inch x 14-inch) rectangle and about 2mm (⅛-inch) thick. Transfer cracker on paper to a large oven tray; remove top sheet of baking paper.

4 Using a knife, score dough at 5cm (2-inch) intervals crossways then lengthways to mark out 5cm (2-inch) squares. Sprinkle with extra rosemary leaves and sea salt.

5 Bake crackers for 20 minutes, rotating tray halfway through cooking, or until golden (cover with foil if it starts to overbrown). Cool on tray. Break into pieces along marked lines before serving.

nutritional count per cracker 2.4g total fat (0.4g saturated fat); 121kJ (29 cal); 0.7g carbohydrate; 1.2g protein; 0.1g fibre

tip These crackers will keep in an airtight container for up to 5 days.

CHEWIES

PREP + COOK TIME 40 MINUTES (+ STANDING) MAKES 16

2 cups (180g) rolled oats

1 cup (100g) desiccated coconut

½ cup (80g) wholemeal plain (all-purpose) flour

¼ cup (50g) pepitas (pumpkin seeds)

¼ cup (30g) natural flaked almonds

¼ cup (40g) sultanas

¼ cup (30g) goji berries

¼ cup (35g) dried cranberries

1 teaspoon bicarbonate of soda (baking soda)

¼ teaspoon sea salt flakes

⅓ cup (75g) virgin coconut oil

¾ cup (180ml) rice malt syrup

½ teaspoon vanilla extract (see tips)

2 tablespoons desiccated coconut, extra

2 tablespoons pepitas (pumpkin seeds), extra

1 Preheat oven to 170°C/340°F. Grease a 20cm x 30cm (8-inch x 12-inch) slice pan; line base with baking paper, extending the paper 5cm (2 inches) over short sides of pan.
2 Combine dry ingredients in a large bowl.
3 Place coconut oil and syrup in a small saucepan; bring to the boil. Boil until oil is melted. Remove from heat; stir in extract.
4 Add oil mixture to dry mixture; stir thoroughly to combine (the mixture will be quite stiff, use clean hands to combine well, if necessary). Spoon mixture into pan, pressing down firmly with a spatula or damp hands to level. Sprinkle with extra coconut and extra pepitas.
5 Bake for 25 minutes or until golden. Turn off oven; leave slice in oven for a further 5 minutes to dry out slightly. Remove from oven; leave slice in pan for 15 minutes.
6 Use the baking paper to help lift the slice onto a wire rack. Cool completely. Remove paper, then cut into 16 pieces.

nutritional count per chewie 13.7g total fat (8.7g saturated fat); 1020kJ (244 cal); 26.7g carbohydrate; 4g protein; 2.4g fibre

tips Vanilla extract contains a tiny amount of refined sugar, if you prefer, either use the scraped seeds of a vanilla bean or vanilla bean powder available from health food stores. Chewies will keep in an airtight container for up to 1 week. If they become sticky, place in the oven at 150°C/300°F for 5 minutes; turn the oven off and leave for 5 minutes.

LEMON, CHIA & YOGHURT CAKE POPS

PREP + COOK TIME 1 HOUR (+ STANDING) MAKES 26

You will need a 20-hole (1 tablespoon/ 20ml) silicone cake pop pan (see tips below). These little baked treats are also gluten-free.

100g (3 ounces) unsalted butter, softened

1 cup (220g) norbu (monk fruit sugar)

2 eggs

2 tablespoons greek-style yoghurt

1 tablespoon finely grated lemon rind

2 tablespoons lemon juice

1 cup (135g) gluten-free plain (all-purpose) flour

1½ teaspoons baking powder

½ teaspoon xanthan gum

1 tablespoon black chia seeds

26 lollypop sticks or straws

yoghurt glaze

½ cup (140g) greek-style yoghurt

2 teaspoons natural lemon extract

1 vanilla bean, split lengthways, seeds scraped

½ cup (90g) stevia icing mix

1 Preheat oven to 200°C/400°F.

2 Beat butter and norbu in the small bowl of an electric mixer for 4 minutes or until light and fluffy; beat in eggs, one at a time. Add yoghurt, rind and juice; beat until just combined. Sift in flour, baking powder and xanthan gum; stir with a wooden spoon until combined.

3 Lightly grease the base of a 20-hole (1 tablespoon/20ml) silicone cake pop pan (see tips). Fill only the holes around the edge of one side of the pan with heaped 2 teaspoons of cake batter; the holes will look over full. Place pop lid on top tightly; bake for 18 minutes or until a toothpick inserted through one of the holes comes out clean. Cool in the pan for 2 minutes; then pop cake pops out onto a wire rack. Cool. Repeat with remaining batter. Trim off any ragged edges using scissors.

4 Make yoghurt glaze.

5 Put the empty silicone pan together to become the holder. One at a time, insert a stick into the middle of each cake pop, dip into glaze and sprinkle with chia seeds; place in the holder while you finish the rest. To hold the extra cake pops, pierce holes in an egg carton with a wooden skewer. Serve cake pops in jars to keep them upright.

yoghurt glaze Whisk ingredients in a small bowl.

nutritional count per pop 4.1g total fat (2.4g saturated fat); 337kJ (81 cal); 8.6g carbohydrate; 1g protein; 0.1g fibre

tips Silicon cake pop moulds have two near identical sides to them. One half is filled, while the other with tiny holes at the top forms the lid. To use them the mould is deliberately over filled for the mixture to rise to the other side and form a ball shape. We found even cooking was achieved by only using the perimeter holes. Moulds can be bought from kitchen supply shops and online.

CARAMELISED ONION &
KUMARA TARTE TARTIN

PREP + COOK TIME 2 HOURS (+ REFRIGERATION) SERVES 6

20g (¾ ounce) butter

1 tablespoon olive oil

1 tablespoon pure maple syrup

3 cloves garlic, sliced thinly

½ teaspoon ground nutmeg

1 tablespoon fresh lemon thyme leaves

350g (11 ounces) baby kumara (orange sweet potato), cut into 1cm (½-inch) slices

1 cup (250ml) water

2 sheets puff pastry

1 egg yolk

1 tablespoon milk or water

100g (3 ounces) goat's curd

caramelised onions

20g (¾ ounce) butter

1 tablespoon olive oil

4 medium onions (800g), sliced finely

¼ cup (60ml) balsamic vinegar

2 tablespoons pure maple syrup

1 tablespoon dijon mustard

1 Make caramelised onions.

2 Heat butter, olive oil and maple syrup in a 30cm (12-inch) ovenproof frying pan over medium heat. Add garlic; cook, stirring, for 1 minute. Remove pan from heat. Sprinkle nutmeg and thyme over base of pan; pack kumara slices, in a single layer, on top; season. Pour half the water over kumara. Return pan to heat; cook for 8 minutes or until the water evaporates. Add remaining water; cook a further 8 minutes or until kumara are browned underneath. Remove from heat; cool 5 minutes.

3 Spoon caramelised onions evenly over kumara with the back of a spoon. Set aside in the fridge to cool completely.

4 Preheat oven to 200°C/400°F.

5 Cut each pasty sheet on a diagonal into two triangles. Whisk egg yolk and milk together in a small bowl. Make a larger square with the four triangles, with the longest edges of the triangles forming the outside of the square; use a little egg wash to stick the pastry together. Place the pastry over the tart and trim overhang. Fold, nip and tuck the edges in to form the pastry around the tart. Brush with egg mixture and prick lightly with a fork. Bake for 20 minutes or until crisp and golden. Stand tart in pan for 5 minutes.

6 To serve, place pan over medium heat for 30 seconds to loosen the base then invert onto a wooden board, top with extra lemon thyme and spoonfuls of goat's curd.

caramelised onions Heat butter and oil in a large heavy-based frying pan over a medium heat; cook onion, stirring frequently for 30 minutes or until very soft and golden. Add vinegar, syrup and mustard; cook for 30 minutes over low heat or until caramelised and reduced. Season.

nutritional count per serving 25g total fat (10.7g saturated fat); 1910kJ (456 cal); 49.6g carbohydrate; 9.3g protein; 5.2g fibre

APPLE & SPICE
FREE-FORM TARTS

PREP + COOK TIME 1 HOUR 20 MINUTES
(+ REFRIGERATION) MAKES 6

4 large green apples (800g), peeled, cored, sliced thickly

⅔ cup (90g) coconut sugar, plus extra to dust

¼ cup (40g) white spelt flour

1 teaspoon ground cinnamon

½ teaspoon ground ginger

1 teaspoon ground cardamom

½ teaspoon sea salt flakes

30g (1 ounce) butter, chopped finely

2 tablespoons apple cider vinegar

1 cup (280g) greek-style yoghurt

1 teaspoon finely grated orange rind

spelt pastry

3 cups (450g) white spelt flour

1 vanilla bean, split lengthways, seeds scraped

¼ cup (40g) coconut sugar

½ teaspoon ground nutmeg

½ teaspoon sea salt flakes

200g (6½ ounces) butter, cut into small cubes

2 tablespoons ice-cold water, approximately

1 Make pastry.

2 Place apples, sugar, flour, spices, salt, butter and vinegar in a large bowl; toss to coat.

3 Preheat oven 180°C/350°F. Line two oven trays with baking paper.

4 Cut pastry in half; roll out each piece between two sheets of lightly floured baking paper until 3mm (⅛-inch) thick. Remove top layer of paper. Using a 17cm (6¾-inch) bowl (or plate) as a guide, cut out 3 rounds from each pastry half. Place apple mixture in the centre, leaving a 3cm (1¼-inch) border. Reserve liquid from apple in the bowl. Fold pastry in, pleating it as you go to partially overlap the filling and create an open topped pie.

5 Transfer the pies to oven tray, brush with liquid from apple mixture; bake for 50 minutes or until golden and apples are tender.

6 Meanwhile, combine yoghurt and rind in a small bowl.

7 Using a large metal lifter, carefully transfer pies to plates. Serve with orange yoghurt.

spelt pastry Process flour, vanilla seeds, sugar, nutmeg, salt and butter until mixture resembles crumbs. Add the water; pulse until mixture just forms a dough. Shape into a disc, wrap in plastic wrap; refrigerate for 1 hour.

nutritional count per tart 35g total fat (22g saturated fat); 3093kJ (739 cal); 94g carbohydrate; 11.8g protein; 2.7g fibre

APRICOT & HAZELNUT
CRUMBLE

PREP + COOK TIME 1 HOUR SERVES 4

4 medium apricots (325g)

2 medium pears (460g)

80g (2½ ounces) dried figs

10g (½ ounce) butter

¾ cup (180ml) water

½ cup (125ml) pure maple syrup

¾ cup (60g) quinoa flakes

¼ cup (30g) ground hazelnuts

½ cup (70g) coarsely chopped skinless hazelnuts, roasted

½ teaspoon sea salt flakes

1 cup (280g) greek-style yoghurt

2 teaspoons long thin strips orange rind

1 Preheat oven to 180°C/350°F.

2 Cut apricots in half; remove and discard stones. Cut unpeeled pears in half; remove core and cut each half into three wedges. Remove stem end from figs and quarter.

3 Combine apricot, pear, fig, butter and the water in a medium saucepan over medium heat; cook, stirring occasionally, for 6 minutes or until pears have softened slightly. Transfer fruit mixture to a 1.5 litre (6-cup) ovenproof dish.

4 Combine maple syrup, quinoa flakes, ground hazelnuts, chopped hazelnuts and salt in a medium bowl; sprinkle over fruit.

5 Bake crumble for 45 minutes or until top is lightly golden. Serve warm topped with yoghurt and rind.

nutritional count per serving 22.9g total fat (4.9g saturated fat); 2295kJ (549 cal); 71.5g carbohydrate; 10.6g protein; 9.9g fibre

tip You can swap 3 peaches for the pears and ground almonds for ground hazelnuts, and coarsely chopped almonds for hazelnuts and raw honey for maple syrup.

PEACH & PISTACHIO
CAKE POTS

PREP + COOK TIME 45 MINUTES MAKES 12

4 small peaches (460g), halved

1 cup (280g) greek-style yoghurt

2 medium apples (300g), grated coarsely

2 eggs, beaten lightly

¼ cup (60ml) milk

2 tablespoons raw honey

2 cups (240g) ground almonds

2 teaspoons baking powder

⅓ cup (45g) pistachios, chopped coarsely

1½ tablespoons raw honey, extra

1 Preheat oven to 180°C/350°F. Cut 12 x 12cm (4-inch) squares from baking paper; line 12 x ⅓ cup (80ml) ovenproof pots with paper squares (see tips).
2 Thinly slice three of the peaches. Coarsely chop remaining peach; blend or process to a coarse puree. Fold peach puree through yoghurt in a small bowl; cover and refrigerate until required.
3 Place apple, egg, milk, honey, ground almonds and baking powder in a large bowl; mix until just combined. Spoon mixture into pots; push peach slices 2cm (¾-inch) into the top of the batter.
4 Bake for 30 minutes or until a skewer inserted in the centre comes out clean.
5 Top cakes with pistachios; drizzle with extra honey. Serve warm or at room temperature with peach yoghurt.

nutritional count per cake 13.8g total fat (1.1g saturated fat); 813kJ (194 cal); 10g carbohydrate; 6.3g protein; 3g fibre

tips We used peat seedling pots available from hardware stores and garden nurseries. You can also cook the cakes in a 12-hole (⅓ cup/80ml) muffin pan, lined with baking paper squares. This recipe is best made on day of serving.

GLOSSARY

ACTIVATED BUCKINIS made with buckwheat, which, despite its name, is not actually a wheat, but is a fruit belonging to the same family as strawberries. It's gluten free, high in protein and essential amino acids, and is a rich source of minerals and B vitamins.

AGAVE SYRUP (ah-GAH-vay) also known as agave nectar; a sweetener produced from the agave plant in South Africa and Mexico (a succulent with thick fleshy leaves, each ending generally in a sharp point and having spiny edges; it is the plant from which tequila is made).

ALLSPICE also known as pimento or jamaican pepper; so-named because it tastes like a combination of nutmeg, cumin, clove and cinnamon. Available whole or ground.

ALMONDS

blanched brown skins removed.

ground also called almond meal; almonds are powdered to a coarse flour-like texture.

flaked paper-thin slices.

slivered small pieces cut lengthways.

BAKING PAPER also called parchment paper or baking parchment – is a silicone-coated paper that is primarily used for lining baking pans and oven trays so cooked food doesn't stick.

BEANS

broad (fava) also called windsor and horse beans; available dried, fresh, canned and frozen. Fresh should be peeled twice (discarding the outer long green pod and the beige-green tough inner shell); frozen beans have had their pods removed but the beige shell still needs removal.

cannellini a small white bean similar in appearance and flavour to other white beans (great northern, navy or haricot), all of which can be substituted for the other. Available dried or canned.

white a generic term we use for canned or cannellini, haricot, navy or great northern beans belonging to the same family; all can be used.

BEETROOT (BEETS) also known as red beets; firm, round root vegetable.

BICARBONATE OF SODA (BAKING SODA) a raising agent.

BROCCOLINI a cross between broccoli and chinese kale; it has long asparagus-like stems with a long loose floret, both are completely edible. Resembles broccoli but is milder and sweeter in taste.

BRUISING a cooking term to describe the slight crushing given to aromatic ingredients, particularly garlic and herbs, with the flat side of a heavy knife or cleaver to release flavour and aroma.

BUTTER use salted or unsalted (sweet) butter; 125g is equal to one stick of butter (4 ounces).

BUTTERMILK originally the term given to the slightly sour liquid left after butter was churned from cream, today it is made from no-fat or low-fat milk to which specific bacterial cultures have been added. Despite its name, it is actually low in fat.

CACAO

beans are contained inside the large cacao pod. The beans are used to make cocoa butter, cocoa powder, cocoa solids and chocolate.

cacao (cocoa) butter is rich in saturated fats; about a third is stearic acid, but this acts differently to other saturated fats in that it doesn't raise cholesterol and, in fact, lowers LDL (bad) cholesterol. So this makes it a pretty healthy fat overall.

dutch-processed cacao powder is treated with an alkali to neutralize its acidity; it is darker and more mellow in taste.

nibs can be separated into cocoa butter and powder. Cocoa powder retains many beneficial antioxidants and is an easy way of adding cocoa into your diet without the kilojoules of chocolate.

raw cacao powder is made by removing the cocoa butter using a process known as cold-pressing. It retains more of its nutrients than heat-processed cacao powder; it also has a stronger, slightly bitter, taste.

raw dark chocolate is made using cold-pressed raw cacao beans, that is, without the use of heat. It is high in antioxidants, and has good levels of chromium, iron and magnesium, which support healthy heart function.

CAPERS grey-green buds of a Mediterranean shrub; sold dried and salted or pickled in a vinegar brine. Rinse before using.

CAPSICUM (BELL PEPPER) also called pepper. Comes in many colours: red, green, yellow, orange and purplish-black. Be sure to discard seeds and membranes before use.

CARDAMOM a spice native to India and used extensively in its cuisine; can be purchased in pod, seed or ground form. Has a distinctive aromatic, sweetly rich flavour.

CHEESE

fetta Greek in origin; a crumbly textured goat- or sheep-milk cheese having a sharp, salty taste. Ripened and stored in salted whey; particularly good cubed and tossed into salads.

fetta, persian a soft, creamy fetta marinated in a blend of olive oil, garlic, herbs and spices. It is available from most larger supermarkets.

goat's made from goat's milk, has an earthy, strong taste; available in both soft and firm textures, in various shapes and sizes, and sometimes rolled in ash or herbs.

haloumi a firm, cream-coloured sheep-milk cheese matured in brine; haloumi can be grilled or fried, briefly, without breaking down. Should be eaten while still warm as it becomes tough and rubbery on cooling.

mozzarella soft, spun-curd cheese; originating in southern Italy where it was traditionally made from water-buffalo milk. Is the most popular pizza cheese because of its low melting point and elasticity when heated.

parmesan also called parmigiano; is a hard, grainy cow-milk cheese originating in Italy. Reggiano is the best variety.

pecorino the Italian generic name for cheeses made from sheep milk; hard, white to pale-yellow cheeses. If you can't find it, use parmesan.

ricotta a soft, sweet, moist, white cow-milk cheese with a low fat content and a slightly grainy texture. The name roughly translates as 'cooked again' and refers to ricotta's manufacture from a whey that is itself a by-product of other cheese making.

CHICKPEAS (GARBANZO BEANS) an irregularly round, sandy-coloured legume. Has a firm texture even after cooking, a floury mouth-feel and robust nutty flavour; available canned or dried (reconstitute for several hours in cold water before use).

CHILLI available in many different types and sizes. Use rubber gloves when seeding and chopping fresh chillies as they can burn your skin. Removing seeds and membranes lessens the heat level.

cayenne pepper a long, thin-fleshed, extremely hot red chilli usually sold dried and ground.

green any unripened chilli; also some particular varieties that are ripe when green, such as jalapeño, habanero, poblano or serrano.

long available both fresh and dried; a generic term used for any moderately hot, thin, long (6-8cm/2¼-3¼ inch) chilli.

red thai also known as 'scuds'; small, very hot and bright red; can be substituted with fresh serrano or habanero chillies.

CHINESE COOKING WINE (SHAO HSING) also known as chinese rice wine; made from fermented rice, wheat, sugar and salt with a 13.5% alcohol content. Inexpensive and found in Asian food shops; if you can't find it, replace with mirin or sherry.

CHINESE FIVE-SPICE POWDER a fragrant mixture of ground cinnamon, cloves, star anise, sichuan pepper and fennel seeds.

CINNAMON available in sticks (quills) and ground into powder; used as a sweet, fragrant flavouring in sweet and savoury foods.

COCOA POWDER also known as cocoa; dried, unsweetened, roasted and ground cocoa beans (cacao seeds).

COCONUT

cream comes from the first pressing of the coconut flesh, without the addition of water; the second pressing (less rich) is sold as coconut milk. Look for coconut cream labelled as 100% coconut, without added emulsifiers.

flaked dried flaked coconut flesh.

flour is a low carbohydrate, high fibre, gluten-free flour made from fresh dried coconut flesh. It has a sweetish taste and is suitable for those on a paleo diet.

milk not the liquid found inside the fruit (coconut water), but the diluted liquid from the second pressing of the white flesh of a mature coconut (the first pressing produces coconut cream).

oil is extracted from the coconut flesh so you don't get any of the fibre, protein or carbohydrates present in the whole coconut. The best quality is virgin coconut oil, which is the oil pressed from the dried coconut flesh, and doesn't include the use of solvents or other refining processes.

shredded thin strips of dried coconut.

sugar is not made from coconuts, but from the sap of the blossoms of the coconut palm tree. The refined sap looks a little like raw or light brown sugar, and has a similar caramel flavour. It also has the same amount of kilojoules as regular table (white) sugar.

water is the liquid from the centre of a young green coconut. It has fewer kilojoules than fruit juice, with no fat or protein. There are sugars present, but these are slowly absorbed giving coconut water a low GI.

young are coconuts that are not fully mature. As a coconut ages, the amount of juice inside decreases, until it eventually disappears and is replaced by air.

CORIANDER (CILANTRO) a bright-green leafy herb with a pungent flavour. Both the stems and roots of coriander are also used in cooking; wash well before using. Also available ground or as seeds; these should not be substituted for fresh coriander as the tastes are completely different.

CREAM

pouring also called pure or fresh cream. It has no additives and contains a minimum fat content of 35%.

thickened (heavy) a whipping cream containing thickener. Minimum fat content 35%.

CRÈME FRAÎCHE a mature, naturally fermented cream (minimum fat content 35 per cent) having a velvety texture and slightly tangy, nutty flavour. Crème fraîche, a French variation of sour cream, can boil without curdling and be used in sweet and savoury dishes.

CUMIN also known as zeera or comino; has a spicy, nutty flavour.

EGGPLANT also known as aubergine. Ranging in size from tiny to very large and in colour from pale green to deep purple.

FENNEL also known as finocchio or anise; a white to very pale green-white, firm, crisp, roundish vegetable about 8-12cm in diameter. The bulb has a slightly sweet, anise flavour but the leaves have a much stronger taste. Also the name given to dried seeds having a licorice flavour.

FISH SAUCE called naam pla (if Thai made) and nuoc naam (if Vietnamese); the two are almost identical. Made from pulverised salted fermented fish (often anchovies); has a pungent smell and strong taste. Available in varying degrees of intensity, so use according to your taste.

FLOUR

chickpea (besan) made from ground chickpeas so is gluten-free and high in protein. Used in Indian cooking.

coconut see Coconut

plain (all-purpose) an all-purpose wheat flour.

self-raising plain flour sifted with baking powder in the proportion of 1 cup flour to 2 teaspoons baking powder.

wholemeal also known as wholewheat flour; milled with the wheat germ so is higher in fibre and more nutritional than plain flour.

GINGER, FRESH also called green or root ginger; thick gnarled root of a tropical plant.

GOJI BERRIES (dried) small, very juicy, sweet red berries that grow on a type of shrub in Tibet. Believed to be high in nutrients and antioxidants.

KAFFIR LIME LEAVES also known as bai magrood. Aromatic leaves of a citrus tree; two glossy dark green leaves joined end to end, forming a rounded hourglass shape. A strip of fresh lime peel may be substituted for each kaffir lime leaf.

KUMARA (ORANGE SWEET POTATO) the Polynesian name of an orange-fleshed sweet potato often confused with yam.

LABNE is a soft cheese made by salting plain (natural) yoghurt and draining it of whey for up to 2 days until it becomes thick enough to roll into small balls, which may be sprinkled with or rolled in chopped herbs or spices.

LEEKS a member of the onion family, the leek resembles a green onion but is much larger and more subtle in flavour. Tender baby or pencil leeks can be eaten whole with minimal cooking but adult leeks are usually trimmed of most of the green tops then sliced.

LEMON GRASS a tall, clumping, lemon-smelling and tasting, sharp-edged aromatic tropical grass; the white lower part of the stem is used, finely chopped. Can be found fresh, dried, powdered and frozen, in supermarkets, greengrocers and Asian food shops.

LENTILS (red, brown, yellow) dried pulses often identified by and named after their colour; also known as dhal.

MAPLE SYRUP, PURE distilled from the sap of sugar maple trees found only in Canada and the USA. Maple-flavoured syrup or pancake syrup is not an adequate substitute for the real thing.

MISO fermented soybean paste. There are many types of miso, each with its own aroma, flavour, colour and texture; it can be kept, airtight, for up to a year in the fridge. Generally, the darker the miso, the saltier the taste and denser the texture. Salt-reduced miso is available. Buy in tubs or plastic packs.

MUSHROOMS, FRESH SHIITAKE also called chinese black, forest or golden oak mushrooms; although cultivated, they are large and meaty and have the earthiness and taste of wild mushrooms.

MUSLIN inexpensive, undyed, finely woven cotton fabric called for in cooking to strain stocks and sauces.

NOODLES, UDON available fresh and dried, these broad, white, wheat Japanese noodles are similar to the ones in home-made chicken noodle soup.

NORI a type of dried seaweed used as a flavouring, garnish or for sushi. Sold in thin sheets, plain or toasted (yaki-nori).

OIL

cooking spray we use a canola oil cooking spray.

olive made from ripened olives. Extra virgin and virgin are the first and second press, respectively, of the olives and are therefore considered the best; the "extra light" or "light" name on other types refers to taste not fat levels.

peanut pressed from ground peanuts; used in Asian cooking because of its capacity to handle high heat without burning.

sesame made from roasted, crushed, white sesame seeds; a flavouring rather than a cooking medium.

vegetable oils sourced from plant rather than animal fats.

ONIONS, GREEN (SCALLIONS) also known as, incorrectly, shallot; an immature onion picked before the bulb has formed. Has a long, bright-green edible stalk.

PEPITAS (PUMPKIN SEEDS) are the pale green kernels of dried pumpkin seeds; they can be bought plain or salted.

PINE NUTS not a nut but a small, cream-coloured kernel from pine cones. They are best roasted before use to bring out the flavour.

POMEGRANATES dark-red, leathery-skinned fresh fruit about the size of an orange filled with hundreds of seeds, each wrapped in an edible lucent-crimson pulp having a unique tangy sweet-sour flavour. To remove the seeds, cut a whole pomegranate in half crossways; hold it, cut-side down, in the palm of your hand over a bowl, then hit the outside firmly with a wooden spoon. The seeds should fall out easily; discard any white pith that falls out with them.

POPPY SEEDS small, dried, bluish-grey seeds of the poppy plant, with a crunchy texture and a nutty flavour. Can be purchased whole or ground in delicatessens and most supermarkets.

QUINOA (KEEN-wa) is a gluten-free grain. It has a delicate, slightly nutty taste and chewy texture. Always rinse well before use.

ROASTING/TOASTING desiccated coconut, pine nuts and sesame seeds roast more evenly if stirred over low heat in a heavy-based frying pan; their natural oils will help turn them golden brown. Remove from pan immediately. Nuts and dried coconut can be roasted in the oven to release their aromatic essential oils. Spread them evenly onto an oven tray then roast at 180°C/350°F for about 5 minutes.

SILVER BEET also known as swiss chard; mistakenly called spinach.

SOY SAUCE made from fermented soy beans. Several variations are available in most supermarkets and Asian food stores. We use japanese soy sauce unless otherwise indicated.

SPINACH also known as english spinach and, incorrectly, silver beet. Baby spinach leaves are best eaten raw in salads; the larger leaves should be added last to soups, stews and stir-fries, and should be cooked until barely wilted.

SUMAC a purple-red, astringent spice ground from berries growing on shrubs that flourish wild around the Mediterranean; adds a tart, lemony flavour to food. Available from spice shops and major supermarkets.

TAHINI a rich, sesame-seed paste, used in most Middle-Eastern cuisines, especially Lebanese, in dips and sauces.

TAMARIND the tamarind tree produces clusters of hairy brown pods, each of which is filled with seeds and a viscous pulp, that are dried and pressed into the blocks of tamarind found in Asian food shops. Gives a sweet-sour, slightly astringent taste to marinades, sauces and dressings.

TURMERIC also called kamin; is a rhizome related to galangal and ginger. Must be grated or pounded to release its acrid aroma and pungent flavour. Known for the golden colour it imparts, fresh turmeric can be replaced with the commonly found dried powder.

VANILLA

bean dried, long, thin pod from a tropical golden orchid; the minuscule black seeds inside the bean impart a luscious flavour in baking and desserts.

extract obtained from vanilla beans infused in water; a non-alcoholic version of essence. Vanilla extract contains a tiny amount of refined sugar; if you prefer, either use the scraped seeds of a vanilla bean or vanilla bean powder available from health food stores

WATERCRESS one of the cress family, a large group of peppery greens. Highly perishable, so must be used as soon as possible after purchase. It has an exceptionally high vitamin K content.

YOGHURT we use plain full-cream yoghurt unless noted otherwise.

greek-style plain yoghurt that has been strained in a cloth (muslin) to remove the whey and to give it a creamy consistency.

ZUCCHINI also called courgette; small, pale- or dark-green or yellow vegetable of the squash family.

CONVERSION CHART

Measures

One Australian metric measuring cup holds approximately 250ml; one Australian metric tablespoon holds 20ml; one Australian metric teaspoon holds 5ml.

The difference between one country's measuring cups and another's is within a two- or three-teaspoon variance, and will not affect your cooking results. North America, New Zealand and the United Kingdom use a 15ml tablespoon.

All cup and spoon measurements are level. The most accurate way of measuring dry ingredients is to weigh them. When measuring liquids, use a clear glass or plastic jug with the metric markings.

The imperial measurements used in these recipes are approximate only. Measurements for cake pans are approximate only. Using same-shaped cake pans of a similar size should not affect the outcome of your baking. We measure the inside top of the cake pan to determine sizes.

We use large eggs with an average weight of 60g.

Dry measures

METRIC	IMPERIAL
15G	½OZ
30G	1OZ
60G	2OZ
90G	3OZ
125G	4OZ (¼LB)
155G	5OZ
185G	6OZ
220G	7OZ
250G	8OZ (½LB)
280G	9OZ
315G	10OZ
345G	11OZ
375G	12OZ (¾LB)
410G	13OZ
440G	14OZ
470G	15OZ
500G	16OZ (1LB)
750G	24OZ (1½LB)
1KG	32OZ (2LB)

Liquid measures

METRIC	IMPERIAL
30ML	1 FLUID OZ
60ML	2 FLUID OZ
100ML	3 FLUID OZ
125ML	4 FLUID OZ
150ML	5 FLUID OZ
190ML	6 FLUID OZ
250ML	8 FLUID OZ
300ML	10 FLUID OZ
500ML	16 FLUID OZ
600ML	20 FLUID OZ
1000ML (1 LITRE)	1¾ PINTS

Length measures

METRIC	IMPERIAL
3MM	⅛IN
6MM	¼IN
1CM	½IN
2CM	¾IN
2.5CM	1IN
5CM	2IN
6CM	2½IN
8CM	3IN
10CM	4IN
13CM	5IN
15CM	6IN
18CM	7IN
20CM	8IN
22CM	9IN
25CM	10IN
28CM	11IN
30CM	12IN (1FT)

Oven temperatures

The oven temperatures in this book are for conventional ovens; if you have a fan-forced oven, decrease the temperature by 10-20 degrees.

	°C (CELSIUS)	°F (FAHRENHEIT)
VERY SLOW	120	250
SLOW	150	300
MODERATELY SLOW	160	325
MODERATE	180	350
MODERATELY HOT	200	400
HOT	220	425
VERY HOT	240	475

INDEX

A

advieh spice mix 73
agave syrup 9
aïoli, lemon 50
amaranth pastry 208
apples
    and spice free-form tarts 228
    apple, rhubarb and goji compote
      22
    cinnamon and fig baked 195
apricot
    and cardamom muesli slice 199
    and hazelnut crumble 231
    and pistachio frozen yoghurt 183
    and tahini bliss balls 106

B

banana
    and choc-almond toastie 28
    and coffee cake with caramel sauce
      200
    pancakes with labne and
      blueberry compote 45
    raw chocolate frozen banana
      treats 179
barbecue sauce, smoky 88
barley malt syrup 8
beetroot
    choc, beetroot and walnut muffins
      211
    relish 60
berry berry luscious 41
bliss balls
    apricot and tahini 106
    date and cacao nibs 106
    fig and hazelnut 106
blood oranges
    fizzed jelly 176
    salad 176
blueberry
    compote 45
    poppy seed crêpes 154
bourbon marinade, sticky 80
breakfast trifle, strawberry and
    passionfruit 16
broad bean tartine 87
brownies, chocolate hazelnut 204
buckwheat waffles with grilled peaches
    188

C

cacao
    and date caramel slice 162
    and hazelnut cookies 192
cake pops, lemon, chia and yoghurt
    224
caramel
    cacao and date slice 162
    date 162
    salted date 110
    sauce 200
    tahini choc cups 168
carrot
    cakes with date cream cheese
      frosting 207
    creamy carrot and miso dip 145
    relish 68
cauliflower
    pizza bites 134
    seeded falafel 67
chai
    chai-spiced popcorn 113
    iced almond chai tea 96
chamomile and lemon sleepy time
    iced tea 97
cheesecake, earl grey and chocolate
    vegan 161
cherry and walnut smoothie 24
chewies 223
chia
    and almond toasted muesli 12
    and tomato guacamole with
      sumac crisps 130
    berry chia seed jam 31
    coconut and berry chia pudding 158
chicken
    fennel, apple and pistachio
      chicken salad 63
    glazed on noodles 93
    honey-roasted hainanese chicken
      rice banquet 64
    olive with maple roasted vegetables
      103
chickpeas and beans, roasted sweet
    and sour 129
chilli
    ginger sauce 64
    green chilli mango and melon
      sorbet 171
    lime snapper with corn salsa salad
      84
    miso soup 125

(*chilli* continued)
    teriyaki marinade 81
    yoghurt 142
chocolate
    banana and choc-almond toastie 28
    choc, beetroot and walnut muffins
      211
    coating 109
    earl grey and chocolate vegan
      cheesecake 161
    hazelnut brownies 204
    hazelnut spread, homemade 114
    hot! hot! hot! 166
    just like a chocolate thick shake...
      40
    raw frozen banana treats 179
    raw power puffs 184
    tahini caramel choc cups 168
coconut
    and berry chia pudding 158
    and mango popsicles 175
    and vanilla muffins 210
    coconut satay sauce 88
    fruit salad 42
    grain-free coconut and vanilla
      muesli 54
    salted, and passionfruit
      semifreddo 157
    sugar 9
cookies, cacao and hazelnut 192
crab
    prawn and crab sweet potato sliders
      100
crêpes, blueberry poppy seed 154
croûtons, pistachio 74
cucumber yoghurt 46
curry, prawn chu chee with
    roti bread 77

D

date
    cream cheese frosting 207
    salted caramels 110
dip, creamy carrot and miso 145
dressings
    healthy caesar 70
    lemon, avocado and dill 71
    maple and dijon 70
    raspberry and white balsamic
      vinaigrette 71
    yoghurt 94